Time as Punishment

Contemporary European Cultural Studies
Gianni Vattimo and Santiago Zabala,
Series Editors

This series publishes English translations of works by contemporary European intellectuals from philosophy, religion, politics, law, ethics, aesthetics, social sciences, and history. Volumes included in this series will not be included simply for their specific subject matter, but also for their ability to interpret, describe, explain, analyze, or suggest theories that recognize its historicity. Proposals and suggestions for this series should be directed to:

The Davies Group Publishers
PO Box 440140
Aurora, Colorado, 80044–0140
US

Manfred Frank, *The Boundaries of Agreement*
Antonio Livi, *Reasons for Believing*
Jósef Ni nik, *The Arbitrariness of Philosophy*
Paolo Crocchiolo, *The Amorous Tinder*
José Guimón, *Art and Madness*
Darío Antiseri, *Poppers Vienna*
Remo Bodei, *Logics of Delusion*
Philip Larrey, *Thinking Logically*
Giovanni Mari, *The Postmodern, Democracy, History*
Emanuela Fornari, *Modernity Out of Joint*
Ana Messuti, *Time As Punishment*
Duncan Kennedy, *Legal Reasoning: Collected Essays*

Time As Punishment

Ana Messuti

A volume in the series
Contemporary European Cultural Studies
Gianni Vattimo and Santiago Zabala, Editors.

The Davies Group, Publishers
Aurora, Colorado

Previously published as *El tiempo como pena*, Campomanes, Buenos Aires, 2001.

Library of Congress Cataloging-in-Publication Data

Messuti, Ana.
[Tiempo como pena. English]
Time as punishment / Ana Messuti.
p. cm. -- (Contemporary european cultural studies)
"Previously published as El tiempo como pena, Campomanes, Buenos Aires, 2001."
Includes bibliographical references.
ISBN-13: 978-1-934542-00-2 (alk. paper)
1. Imprisonment. 2. Punishment--Philosophy. I. Title.
K5105.M47 2008
345'.077--dc22

2007047851

Printed in the United States of America
Published 2008. The Davies Group Publishers, Aurora, CO

1234567890

Contents

Foreword

In every discipline there are certain spheres of straight contiguity with other disciplines, spheres where if one proceeds while ignoring such contiguity one runs the risk of stifling the discipline, of closing an avenue of communication that would not only enrich it but would also provide the necessary perspective for such a discipline to understand itself.

In philosophy, one of the most disquieting and profound topics is time. In law, one of the primary objectives is the temporal continuity of the relationships it regulates. For criminal law, time is the measurement of a punishment that has virtually become the punishment *par excellence*: imprisonment. And, closing the circle, in philosophy of law one of the most contentious disciplines, one most deserving of reflection, is criminal law. All these perspectives converge upon the human being, whose temporality is indeed his life.

I approach the relationship between time and punishment from a retributive point of view because only this perspective offers clarity in the analysis of the measurement of punishment, the guiding thread that runs through all these papers. I have started off from the measurement of punishment, the calculation of the duration of punishment, from the calculative thought itself, so that this manner of thinking, the acceptable, necessary thinking of our everyday lives, may lead us to another kind of thought, meditative thinking, which goes deeper.

Perhaps my contribution will be limited to pointing out the philosophical dimension of criminal law and the need to ponder the ethical problems it raises. For there is no doubt that if there is a branch of law directly adjacent to philosophy, one calling out for the illumination of philosophical thought, it is criminal law.

Ana Messuti
November, 2007

Chapter One

Time As Punishment

Punishment and Retribution

The fact that so many theories seek to justify punishment makes clear the profound problem of conscience caused by this institution. Punishment is an example of "bad conscience." It is natural that harming others should give rise to a feeling of guilt and with it the need to explain the reasoning behind such behavior. Practically all the theories that have been developed in connection with punishment seek to justify it by demonstrating that it is but a means leading to an end generally understood to be good.

Punishment relates, however, to feelings as deep-rooted as the feeling of guilt that it appears to awaken. Benveniste points out that the origin of the term "punishment" in Greek was *poine*, which accorded exactly with the meaning of "vengeance" and "hatred," namely, retribution designed to compensate for a crime, expiation by blood. Hence, there is also an emotional shift towards hatred and retaliation understood as retribution.[1]

The concept of retribution is of fundamental importance to social life; it corresponds to the basic structure of human interchange, without which no social life would be possible. A gift invites a countergift. If it is accepted as a matter of course that giving something characterized as positive should lead to something deemed positive being reciprocated, then it must also be accepted that an act of giving something negative will result in a negative reciprocation.

If the punishment is based on exchange, as an integral part of it, that is to say, as one of the acts of reciprocation, then it must be considered that punishment *is given* and not *applied*. The latter would be valid in a subject-object relation, where the subject would apply something to the object. Between two subjects, however, it is possible only that one gives and the other receives, or vice versa. Giving and receiving have a common etymological root: Benveniste considers that this root, "do," means neither exactly to give nor exactly to receive but rather one or the other, depending on the construction of the term.[2] Just as in commerce giving and receiving follow one another in harmony, so too in society and law.

The reciprocity of the gift is a notion so fundamental to our social life that we find it at the very heart of the word *community*. In *munus* we find the concept of duty and function, but also favour, and *com-munis* literally means "that partakes in the *munia* or *munera*."[3] There is an obligation to give to the extent that one receives, and it is those who partake in this giving and receiving who make up the community. The idea of retribution is therefore inherent in social life. It responds to a precise symmetry of reciprocation that makes it possible for the system to remain in equilibrium. In establishing standards of conduct among individuals this symmetry must at all times be observed.

Accordingly, when one person has harmed another, making amends for the damage done is imperative. A human community, though, is not a mechanical but a social system. It has a history, and since history is irreversible, it cannot go back in time; things cannot simply be put back in their earlier place; symmetry cannot simply be restored by a return to an earlier situation.[4]

Nevertheless, even if such amends were fully practicable, the lost equilibrium would be only partially restored. For unless it represented at the same time a punishment of the perpetrator of the crime, the restitution in itself would not be sufficient to restore the lost equilibrium. Nor would it be simply a question of interpersonal relationships: not only would the crime constitute harm against one member of the community of persons, but it would also cause injury to the law of that community. It would alter the balance at two levels, individual and public. Reparation would belong to the former, retribution to the latter.

Such a purely legal notion of punishment, that is, a notion exempt from any value outside the actual violation of the law, is shared, for instance, by Hegel: "everything turns on the point that in crime it is not the production of evil but the injury of right as right, which must be set aside and overcome. We must ask what that is in crime, whose existence has to be removed. That is the only evil to be set aside, and the essential thing is to determine wherein that evil lies."[5] In other words, crime must be eliminated, irrespective of the actual damage it may have caused, because it is harmful in and of itself. Making amends for its consequences does not constitute punishment. There could be a de facto coincidence of making amends and punishment but never a conceptual one. For this reason Nietzsche's query about whether "making suffer" could possibly make amends[6] could be answered by stating that "making suffer" is aimed not at reparation but rather at punishment.

Hence it is necessary to draw a distinction between the concept of restitution and that of retribution. The main goal of retribution seems to be to reaffirm a certain state of affairs regarded as just, adequate, or simply desirable, one, which has been threatened or modified by an unwanted act.[7]

As a consequence of the crime, a prevailing state of affairs has been not only threatened but actually disrupted. Retribution aims to restore a fair equilibrium, considered as a function of what happens to the agent, rather than in terms of restitution to the victim.[8]

The distinction between what pertains to the injured party and what pertains to the criminal is essential for the definition of punishment. What pertains to the victim is based on his right to receive compensation for the harm done to him. Punishment as it pertains to the criminal is also based on a right which at the same time is a duty: it is no longer that of the victim, however, but that of the community of persons. For the community as such becomes the indirect recipient of any injury caused to a single individual, since it believes that such an injury represents a threat to the entire society. Not only is "what is restored to the victim" important but also, and most especially, "what happens to the agent," the author of the crime.

And what happens to the author of the crime is precisely punishment, punishment as retribution from a community of persons which deems itself threatened by his actions. This retribution is negative, since its intention is to cancel out the crime.

If retribution as a reaction has its origin in harm done to another, is it not contradictory that the same community, through punishment, should itself then do harm to the person of the offender? Durkheim considers this paradox to be one reason for reducing the severity of the punishment. In his view there is a true and irremediable contradiction in taking vengeance for the lost dignity of the offended person by then violating the dignity of the offender himself.[9] However, according to Durkheim as well, this irremediable contradiction, insofar as it cannot be eliminated, has led to more lenient punishment, for the offender, as a person, deserves also the respect of the community of persons. A possible solution would be to consider retribution not as a "violation" of the criminal's "dignity," but rather as the opposite, as an expression of respect for it by considering him a rational being who receives what he deserves on the basis of his actions. This solution would justify punishment as a function of the symmetry necessary to social life.

Moreover, such a "violation of human dignity," to use Durkheim's own words, constitutes, above all, the denial of a will. From a retributive point of view the negation of such a will is essential to the existence of the community of persons, since this will has revealed itself to be contrary to it. The community of persons must reassert itself before any manifestation of a will that would seek to negate it, and it must do so with a uniform, unique, and final response. The community's counteraction is the last link in the chain: it does not lead to further action. This quality of the final word is born of the inequality between the subjects in the exchange involved in punishment."You were not on an equal footing with your father as regards the right, nor with your master if you had one, so as to retaliate for anything they did to you, to revile them if they reviled you, to beat them if they beat you .... Do you think you have this right to retaliation against your country and its laws?"[10]

There is no equality of rights between the community of persons and each one of its members. When society "strikes," there is no "strike" in return. This is why punishment is punishment and not revenge.

Revenge carries with it the danger of yet another unequal relationship, not one between subjects but rather one between actions. For revenge is exerted by the offended, and injury appears to him not within its quantitative and qualitative limits but just as injury in general; he may therefore overdo his retribution and thus give rise to further injury.[11] Thus, one raison d'être of this relationship involving punishment is that retribution needs to respect certain qualitative and quantitative rules, so that there may be reciprocation, rather than further action that could bear no relation to the initial action.

I. Measure

Benveniste points out that the root *med* refers not to measure in the sense of measurement (for which we have the root *me*, from which *mensis*, "month," "measure of dimension," are derived) but to measure that is imposed on things. This is not about "*metior*," but about "*moderari*," that is, subjecting to measure. Comparing it with the meaning of measure in the sense of dimension, he says: "We see something very different in '*modus*': a measure of constriction, which presupposes reflection, premeditation, and which is applied to a disorderly situation."[12] This definition contains several elements: limitation, reflection, and deliberation, on the one hand, and a disorderly situation on the other.

The topic that concerns us, the disorderly situation that crime, by its mere existence, has provoked, requires that the counteraction should be the product of deliberation and reflection, like an answer to a question. Merely by being an answer, a reciprocation, punishment contains within itself an element of measure. But in addition it seeks to impose measure, to subject a certain situation to measure; not an arbitrary measure, however, but a pre-established one. This is why we can say, following Cotta, that punishment is an act that encompasses three kinds of measure, namely, one that is intrinsic to the act, whereby the action carries with it a certain measure; one that is external, whereby action takes place according to a certain measure; and finally, one which the act is intended to introduce.[13]

Cotta refers to punishment as an act that encompasses these three types of measure because, since it would have followed established procedure, it would evidently have been subject to certain limits and would thus itself be a self-measuring act (*atto automisurantesi*). He indicates, however, that this quality would also have derived from the need to maintain some proportion in relation to the acts to which it would have responded. The second kind of measure, according to which the act would have been performed, would have derived from the rules of criminal law (the *misura externa all'atto*). There would also have been a measure directed towards an end, namely, a measure to restore balance.[14]

The act of punishment is thus distinguished from the act that precedes it, even though externally they may appear to be identical. Like sacrifice, it is a violent act; its violence, however, is not equal to the destructiveness that provokes it. "Nothing could seem more alike than two drops of blood, yet in this case nothing could be more different." The metaphor used by Girard to refer to sacrifice can also be applied to punishment. The same substance both pollutes and purifies; there is an apparent identity between ill and remedy.[15] But despite this apparent identity, punishment and crime are opposites, by virtue of the presence or absence of *measure*, which is also *moderari*: re-establishing an equilibrium. Wherever the responding action is lacking, there remains an imbalance that must be corrected in order to re-establish the lost normality. Indeed, the measure of the act embodying punishment is partly established by its relationship to the crime.

II. Relationship Between Crime and Punishment

The simplest manifestation of the relationship between crime and punishment would be the talion. However, from a practical point of view, this leads to absurd situations (theft for theft, robbery for robbery, an eye for an eye, a tooth for a tooth …). This difficulty, which comes from a search for equality between acts, appears also in the exchange forming the foundation of society. Exchange requires an intellectual act extending beyond the external appearance of things and actions, in order to find an element that makes comparison possible. There is a need to overcome specific equality and the immediate nature of the thing. "Only when we limit ourselves to equality in the external details are theft and robbery unequal to fine and imprisonment. But from the standpoint of their value and the general capacity to be injuries, they can be equated."[16]

Indeed, it is possible to interchange crime and punishment precisely because they both have a negative value: their general property of being injuries. That is why punishment as retribution for damage can be nothing but harmful. Otherwise how could one possibly compare an injury to a good?

Nevertheless, once we have found the common element that allows us to establish a relationship of exchange, it is necessary to find a proportion between such actions, and as we have seen, such proportion cannot be based on mere equality. Punishment consists of an act with a measure that is defined, among other things, by its proportion to the act that preceded and caused it.[17] "If geometry were adaptable to the infinite and obscure combinations of human activity, there ought to be a corresponding scale of punishments, descending from the most rigorous to the slightest";[18] such was Beccaria's advice. Nevertheless, what has occurred is exactly the opposite: the responses to a great variety of acts that may be considered crimes have become more and more uniform over time, practically being reduced to just one. Once their internal equality, i.e., their general property of being injuries, is revealed, the response to the great diversity of injuries that may be considered crimes will almost invariably be found to be the same: "So that if I have betrayed my country, I go to prison; if I have killed my father, I go to prison; every imaginable offence is punished in the same uniform way. One might as well see a physician who has the same remedy for all ills."[19]

A phenomenon similar to the emergence of currency in commerce has occurred. In this respect Foucault points out that prison offers a certain legal clarity, since it allows for the exact quantification of punishment in relation to time. "There is a wages-form of imprisonment that constitutes, in industrial societies, its economic 'self-evidence' - and enables it to appear as a reparation." Indeed, by taking possession of the convict's time, prison appears to give expression to the notion that the crime has injured not only the victim but also the entire society. "There is an economic-moral self-evidence of a penalty that metes out punishments in days, months and years, and draws up quantitative equivalences between offences and duration."[20]

III. Punishment by Imprisonment

The following is Hobbes' definition of punishment by imprisonment: "Under this word, Imprisonment, I comprehend all restraint of motion, caused by an external obstacle."[21] This broad definition includes, as he subsequently explains, not just imprisonment but also deportation, hard labor in mines or quarries, galleys, or simply chains. Here I will deal only with imprisonment, strictly speaking, which is the only punishment to have endured, creating a uniformity that has resulted also in the uniformity of the "external obstacle" that restrains the freedom of motion: the prison walls.

IV. The Place

Durkheim links the availability of locations intended to become prisons to the development of certain conditions that allowed for the existence of public buildings that were sufficiently large, were militarily occupied, and were organized in such a way as to prevent all external communication. These conditions occur once collective life has reached a certain intensity and continuity and when the line that separates authority from its subjects begins to appear in the distribution of social space.[22] He indicates that the three prisons that existed in Jerusalem when the Chaldeans invaded the city were situated at the high gate of Benjamin, at the king's palace, and at the residence of a public officer. In Rome, too, the earliest prisons were located in the royal fortress.

It makes sense that the site of punishment should be under the direct supervision of those possessing the authority to execute it. Durkheim indicates, however, that during the period to which he refers, prison still had the purely preventive purpose of holding a person who was presumed guilty (although the living conditions inside were so bad as to constitute true punishment).[23] In this connection, there is an interesting passage in Plato's *Laws* describing three kinds of prisons, each with a specific function:

"The State will have three prisons: (1) a public one near the market-place for the general run of offenders, where large numbers may be kept in safe custody; (2) one called the 'reform center,' near the place where the Nocturnal Council assembles; and (3) another in the heart of the countryside, in a solitary spot where the terrain is at its wildest, and the title of this prison is somehow to convey the notion of 'punishment.'"[24]

In the first prison, "where large numbers [of offenders] may be kept in safe custody," the goal was safety, the prevention of further crimes. Passage 909a determines who would be lodged in the other two: "those who have simply fallen victim to foolishness and who do not have a bad character and disposition *should be sent* to the reform center": In other words, those who could be redeemed. The corrective function was entrusted to the officers of the Nocturnal Council. Evidently, this prison had not a punitive but rather a corrective character. Instead, the punitive function was assigned to the last of the three prisons, which was intended for "others, however, who in addition to not recognizing the existence of the gods ... become subhuman."

Thus, the distinction between the first two prisons depends on the seriousness of the crime or the criminal tendencies of the offender, and it is marked by the location chosen for the prisons. To the exclusively punitive prison, "a solitary spot where the terrain is at its wildest" is assigned.

A similar situation is found in the spatial organization of Dante's inferno. "Ei son tra l'anime più nere; diverse colpe giù li grava al fondo." A note explains that an analogy is being drawn here between the law of gravity in physics, "tutti i corpi gravitano verso il centro dell terra," and the law of moral gravity, "i peccati sono puniti in ordiner di gravità, dall' alto al basso."[25] It is also present in Song IX, in reference to the Giudecca: "Quell' è'l più basso loco e'l più oscuro, / e'l più lontan dal ciel che tutto gira." For the Giudecca corresponds to the center of the Earth and is the lowest point, not only material but also moral, since the seriousness of the sins increases from top to bottom. In the Giudecca one finds maximum punishment and deprivation of God (light), that is, extreme darkness. The greatest spiritual distance thus corresponds to the greatest material distance, taking the sky as the point of reference, or the place thought to be closest to God.[26] This spatial dimension of punishment assigns a fundamental importance to the locus of its execution. The more serious the crime, the farther away is the criminal's space. In our earthly punishment, the community takes on the role of light, which in Dante is attributed to God. Similarly, in Plato the punitive prison entails the total isolation of the offender from the rest of the community of persons. The desire to set him apart (so as not to have contact with free men) is evident. At first sight, the only certain thing about this punitive prison is the exclusion from the community of persons. This is borne out by the fact that not even death would bring an end to this exclusion, since "[w]hen he dies the body must be cast out over the borders of the state unburied. "[27]

Gernet refers to forms of punishment which are in themselves and above all religious and which aim at removing a stain or which assume the notion of the consecration of the culprit, who is relinquished by the community to divine powers, so that the community itself may be delivered from these powers.[28] Outside the borders there is an unknown territory, an area ruled not by order but by chaos. The borders indicate a break in space: the inhabited, organized territory ("our world") and a space that does not belong to the community of persons, that remains at the mercy of divine powers.[29] Thanks to technology, however, the human being has made all Earth a cosmos. There is no chaos left on Earth. The "world," "our world," reaches out to every corner. Yet the walls that were constructed to separate cosmos from chaos did not fulfill just a protective role. Above all, their role consisted in distinguishing between these two territories and between those inhabiting one or the other of them.

An absence of chaos would suggest that this space was one and the same, without differentiation or limit. However, a limit is not where something comes to an end but rather where it begins to exist. If the social space were to lose the limits that separate it from chaos it would no longer be the social space.

A fundamental need for the social space to differentiate itself in order to maintain its identity, arising from the limits within which it has come into existence, leads it to construct its own chaos. The prison is the chaos that the community has built for itself. One could argue that chaos has always been associated with a lawless, disorderly territory and that prison, quite to the contrary, is governed by much stricter rules than the social space. Nevertheless, one must not forget that this is chaos that has been constructed for a very specific purpose. It is chaos insofar as it is "non-cosmos," and its disorder, in the sense of lack of harmony, consists precisely in an intensification of the rigor of the norm. As opposed to the original chaos, which implied a total lack of rules, the constructed chaos implies an excessive set of rules; rules aimed at achieving not the harmony of cohabitation but the stiffness of immobility.

Just as a geographical border demarcates two territories, so do prison walls inside a city. A prison is characterized, above all, by a minimum of communication with the outer social world. What makes it a prison is the impossibility of walking freely through its doors: its walls mark a break in the social space. Although apparently, with respect to its general location, a prison is not usually separated from, isolated from, or located outside the urban area, as is the case, for example, with cemeteries, any communication between it and the society that surrounds it is much more restricted than in the case of cemeteries. Plato's punitive prison would therefore be placed in the wildest and most isolated site, outside the city limits. Even though today we might often find a prison in the centre of an urban area, it will always be, to the observer, the wildest and most isolated place in the city.

It is interesting to interpret this phenomenon of exclusion as a symbolic act of reproof. The community of persons has nothing to do with the author of certain acts. If it were to tolerate his presence or if a coexistence with him persisted, such tolerance and coexistence could be interpreted as acceptance. And acceptance is not far from complicity. A positive stand could thus be inferred from a merely passive attitude. "Punishment is a conventional device for the expression of attitudes of resentment and indignation, on the part either of the punishing authority himself or of those 'in whose name' the punishment is inflicted. Punishment, in short, has a symbolic significance largely missing from other kinds of penalties."[30]

The symbolic meaning of punishment does not exhaust itself in the manifestation of reproof, however, but stretches out to the individualization of those who deserve reproof. In this regard, the reasoning "he is in jail because he is a criminal" would be inverted to "he is a criminal because he is in jail." Nevertheless, what is sought in both cases – the expression of reproof and the individualization of criminals – is to reassert the innocence of the community of persons.

Prison walls separate those who are innocent from those who are not. One can then wonder whether those who are outside those walls are truly innocent. If one assigns a negative definition to the term, that is, if only those who have not violated the law are considered to be innocent, then this classification is possible. But if we adopt a positive definition of innocence, understanding it primarily as trustworthiness – and this on two separate grounds: because the innocent trusts the others but at the same time because he gives himself to the others, whom he trusts[31] - then the people of the community of persons that coexist outside the prison walls cannot be considered to be innocent either. Evidently, they do not trust the others. This is not about distrusting them *a posteriori* because others have committed crimes but about distrusting them *a priori* because they too can be expected to commit crimes. Thus, punishment symbolizes a lack of innocence in society.[32]

From an equally symbolic perspective punishment could be considered a talion. The criminal has disrupted the flow of social communication proper to the community, and as a consequence, that is, as a form of retribution, he will be deprived of the social communication that he has disrupted.

Of course, if punishment were nothing besides its symbolic content, one could ask, along with Feinberg: "Now we condemn felons to penal servitude as the way of rendering their crimes infamous. Could not the job be done still more economically? Isn't there a way to stigmatize without inflicting any further (pointless) pain to the body, to family, to creative capacity?"[33] However, punishment does not have an exclusively symbolic function: it is also intended to inflict an ill, to chastise.

V. Time

Just as there is a rupture in the social space marked out by the prison walls, so there is a rupture, too, in time.

Punishment by imprisonment differs from all other forms of punishment in the way it combines these two elements: time and space. This intersection of time and space marks the beginning of another kind of duration, which is qualitatively different. This is so despite the fact that punishment is measured with the same unit that is also used to measure social time, public time.

Punishment by imprisonment cannot be defined exclusively as a physical separation. When referring to this type of punishment, one normally asks, "how long," because its true significance is in terms of time rather than space. There is a great difference between spending a few days or an entire life in prison: there is an entire life of difference. A prison is constructed to fix the time of punishment, to dissociate it from the social time that goes by in the social space. A prison is a spatial construction used to calculate time in a special manner. The stiffness of space is opposed to the flowing of time. By means of the prison, the legal system seeks to control time. It would seem as though the time in which normal social life develops was a relative time, whereas the time of punishment, which exists inside a prison, assumes an absolute character. "In space everything is fixed and clear in the geometry of proportions; everything flows and goes by in the rhythm of time."[34]

This use of time made by the law is very peculiar. If punishment is retribution and punishment by imprisonment mainly consists of serving time, then what is being used as punishment is time itself. This is not the only example of a bizarre interpretation of time in criminal law. Gernet, for instance, recalls the concept of flagrancy. This was not considered a privileged type of evidence but formed a part of the concept of crime itself.[35] If the crime was a flagrant act, that is, if it appeared to be a deliberate flouting of the law, it led to the immediate execution of punishment. Whatever had occurred became present. This unity, this continuity, condensed in time, in the present, represented an ideal for criminal law: the possibility that a sanction and a criminal act could be one and the same, a seamless unit. Everything happens in the present, at the same time, without any intervention of the notion of past time, not even of the recent past.[36] This disregard for the past, or the wish to disregard the past, can also be observed in the notion of *furtum*, which referred to the stolen object. When a criminal was found in possession of the *furtum*, it was not necessary to go back in time to prove what had occurred earlier. The operation or administration of time by the law went even further: archaic law assimilated the notion of a flagrant crime into that of a crime made evident by the discovery of the stolen object in the offender's living quarters. In this case there was a temporal distance, in that the crime could not be proven at the "exact moment" in which it had occurred. However, by means of a fictional operation, this temporal gap would vanish; the intervening time counted for nothing.[37]

The ideal of continuity between crime and punishment persists. Beccaria recommends it, although he does so in relation to the exemplary role that he attributes to punishment. Indeed, he points out "that promptness of punishment is more useful, for the less time passes between the misdeed and its chastisement, the stronger and more permanent is the human mind's association of the two ideas of *crime* and *punishment*, so that imperceptibly the one will come to be considered as the cause, and the other as the necessary and inevitable result."[38]

An aversion to digging into the past likewise persists: "Can the cries of a poor wretch turn back time and undo actions which have already been done?" wondered Beccaria.[39] Punishment and pain cannot undo what has been done. Nothing can be done by man to change what has already taken place, what no longer belongs to man because it already forms a part of the past. As Mathieu points out, however, punishment is absurd from a purely temporal perspective, as is evident in the phrase "what is done is done." It is rather that punishment, to his mind, takes on the totality of past, present, and future acts as a whole and aims at making this whole respond, if possible, into a universal principle of justice whereby what has not yet come into existence might compensate for what no longer exists, what has been might weigh as if it were present, and lastly, even what should have existed but never did might likewise be of influence in establishing balance.[40]

VI. Another Kind of Measure

How can one determine the relative value of something pleasurable or painful other than by making a quantitative estimate? The concept of this pleasure as determined by a plus or minus is defined in *Protagoras,* where a true "science of measurement" (*metrètikè technè*) is discussed. It is the science of excess and defect (also called Arithmetic, the art of measurement, by Plato).[41] True wisdom allows man to choose between good and evil, between pleasure and pain, applying a quantitative criterion. Such is the importance attributed to measurement in this dialogue, that it is also referred to as the salvation of our life, since our salvation is contingent upon making the right choice between pleasure and pain, accurately appraising what is plentiful or scarce, greater or lesser, closer or remote.

This possibility of quantifying pleasure or pain by estimating a plus or a minus is also an element of punishment, since in order to establish its proper relationship to crime, it is necessary to compare them both. But this comparison cannot be qualitative only (based on both crime and punishment being injuries). In order for a punishment to be an act "with measure," it must be proportional to the crime. Such proportion can be ascertained only by measuring the intensity of both acts. Nevertheless, we are dealing no longer with measure as the quality of an act but rather with measure of a different meaning altogether. Indeed, its root is not *med* but *me.* The verb is not *moderari* but *metior.* In addition, from *me* are derived *mens,* "moon," and in Latin, as mentioned above, *mensis,* "month," a measure of dimension: "a fixed and kind of passive quality, symbol of which will be the moon measuring the month."[42] This would be the ordinary meaning of the verb "to measure," not the sense of subjecting something to a measure but that of quantifying it.

As opposed to space, which in itself is something that is measurable, that is seen to be something to be measured, time appears to us as already bearing its own natural measure, as something already divided into parts in the flow of seasons and days and in "the movement of the celestial clock that nature, in all its wisdom, has put at our disposal."[43]Measuring time is not the same as measuring space, therefore, since time has an intrinsic measure of its own in the sense that, as we have seen, it already appears, it presents itself, in a way, divided into parts that follow one upon another. The use of instruments to measure time is aimed at achieving a certain precision and accuracy in the subdivision of those parts. Koyré points out that only when urban civilizations experience the need for precision in their public and religious life does time begin to be measured.

Even though the Bible teaches us that God created the world on the basis of "number, weight, and measure," until Galileo's time nobody had tried to use number, weight, and measure to overcome the imprecision of everyday life.[44] But when the deprivation of freedom assumes the attribute of punishment (as opposed to prevention, correction, or any other social health goal) the need for precision becomes manifest. Insofar as time is the essential element of punishment, it cannot be open to inaccuracy. The temporal determination of punishment acquires fundamental importance.

VII. Crime and Time

The plus or minus of the injury involved in punishment by imprisonment is its duration. This is why Beccaria says, "It is not the severity of punishment that has the greatest impact on the human mind, but rather its duration, for our sensibility is more easily and surely stimulated by tiny and repeated impressions than by a strong but temporary movement."[45] But this "duration" must correspond to a specific "intensity"; otherwise it would not be possible to compare it to the crime, which is an injury of a certain seriousness, which could just as well be called "intensity." It is necessary to measure the intensity of both. If the punishment is measured by its duration, what is the corresponding "intensity" in terms of a specific duration?

What is the relationship between time and crime? Obviously a crime is not measured by how long it lasts. In book 21, chapter 11, of *The City of God*, under the title "Whether It Is Just that the Punishments of Sins Last Longer than the Sins Themselves Lasted," Saint Augustine responds to those who believe that it is fair to punish the sins committed in this short life, whatever their seriousness, with eternal suffering: "As if any law ever regulated the duration of the punishment by the duration of the offence punished!"[46] Saint Augustine also refers to the duration of imprisonment by indicating the absurdity of quantifying punishment according to the duration of the crime, since in order to determine its seriousness, other criteria are applied than the criterion of how long it took to be perpetrated.[47]

It is interesting to note that in the same chapter, a little further on, Saint Augustine refers to the time-punishment relationship: on the one hand, he observes that there is no relationship between the duration of an offence and the duration of its punishment; on the other hand, just as the worst crime may be committed in an instant, so the most serious punishment may also be applied in an instant. In other words, the duration of the application of punishment does not indicate its seriousness. Saint Augustine gives capital punishment as evidence of this. Nevertheless, a time element is introduced once punishment is regarded as an *everlasting* separation of a criminal from human society. This "everlasting" element provides an answer to the question of how long we want to keep him apart from society. The death sentence is precisely capital punishment because the answer is forever.

VIII. Prison and Death

This reference to capital punishment might allow us to draw a parallel with the penalty of imprisonment. Is not the separation sought by means of imprisonment comparable to that achieved, in a final manner, by death? The immediate effect of both is expulsion. In the present, they both have the same meaning: exclusion. They differ only as regards their future consequences. However, according to Saint Augustine such future consequences, belonging as they do to the future, "do not yet exist, and if they are not yet present, they do not exist; and if they have no being, they cannot be seen at all. But they can be predicted from present events which are already present and can be seen."[48]

In one, a possible return can be anticipated in the present; but in the other, such a possibility is excluded. Therefore punishment by imprisonment differs from capital punishment through the possibility or not of being reincorporated into social coexistence.

However, they both disrupt such coexistence in the present.

When are two beings said to coexist or to exist at the same time? When they do not succeed each other, when they both exist: when the existence of one and the negation of the other do not occur at the same time. Both in capital punishment and in punishment by imprisonment there is a "negation of the other." The subject is negated by separation, from the wish that he not continue to exist in the present time of everyone.

To what extent can we consider that both punishments differ only in their quantitative element that is, in that the duration of the one is much greater than that of the other? From the perspective of the subjects from whose existence the criminal has been removed, the "forever" of capital punishment simply signifies a longer duration. They will not exist "forever" either, and therefore they will not be able to verify the "forever" of capital punishment.

Both punishments can be compared to two journeys. In one a return is anticipated, indeed expected; in the other, it is not.

If we were to accept this quantitative difference, Gernet's hypothesis would then likewise be acceptable. Analyzing certain defamatory punishments in which the criminal is publicly exposed, Gernet points to temporary and relatively benign punishments that could be regarded as more lenient versions, or symbols, of capital punishment.[49] Although imprisonment involves removal from sight, rather than exposure, given that it has also taken on a defamatory character and is now the form of punishment par excellence, the same hypothesis could be applied to it. It could also be considered a more lenient punishment than capital punishment, the only difference being the quantitative element of its duration. In imprisonment for life or for periods of time that exceed the life span of a human being, the "return," the "rejoining," is not anticipated either. The criminal is excluded "forever," as in the case of death.

In life imprisonment, says Mathieu, the underlying purpose is the same as in capital punishment: "you shall never return among us." According to this author, the meaning of this sentence is perfectly clear: only when dead can you rejoin the system of freedom. However, in order to reach this ultimate state, in life imprisonment nature is allowed to intervene. This is why he calls life imprisonment a "delayed death sentence," and considers it hypocritical that the execution of punishment should be entrusted to the workings of nature and time[50] (and, we could add, to living conditions prevailing in many prisons and likewise to all the many ailments brought on by imprisonment).

In the case of life imprisonment, however, or of sentences of periods longer than the criminal's life expectancy, the eventual death is not considered as a deferred punishment. Such sentences simply respond to the need to measure out a punishment in the sense of quantifying it. Death occurs separately from punishment; the punishment consists of an exclusion that lasts a specific period of time, but it does not consist of death itself. Death might occur during even a brief term of prison. We find in sentences that exceed the criminal's life expectancy absurd because criminal law, in a sense, does not care about what actually takes place in reality. As explained earlier by Mathieu: "The fact is that criminal law considers justice regardless of time and of the succession of processes over time. Punishment must follow a crime as an artificial consequence of it; however, real and therefore temporal processes that form or occur concurrently with punishment are accidental."[51]

Nevertheless, rather than being indifferent to these temporal processes, criminal law, in a certain sense, uses them to its own ends. As Gernet points out, there is on the part of the law some liberty in the use of a concept that it cannot do without but that it adapts to its own purposes. For what matters to criminal law is that the punishment should be proportional to the crime. That is why, even if the subject has no chance of living through the full duration of his punishment, this punishment is determined in such a way as to restore equilibrium, irrespective of the fact that the sentence might not be served in full. It is in this particular aspect, in the way that it is determined, that the symbolic character of punishment is reaffirmed.

M. Foucault,[52] referring to Kantorowicz ("The Two Bodies of the King"), draws a parallel between the body of the king and the body of the convict. In the body of the king, along with the temporary aspect of birth and death, there is another aspect that endures, which is both the physical and the intangible support of the kingdom, the object of an iconography and of a political and juridical doctrine, the foundation of power. At the other extreme, the diminished body of the convict is also the object of a ceremonial, a theoretical discourse, and a juridical construction. According to Foucault, as an excess of power is exerted upon him, a partition takes place. It is as if the law had created a metaphysical division of the body of the criminal in order to subject him to punishments not commensurate with the actual coordinates of his natural body.

The criminal, however, does not outlive his own death. The criminal is not immortal. The community of persons *is* immortal, as it subsists as such despite the changing of the people that make it up. The time of punishment is measured in relation to the community. The time of punishment is quantified as a function of the time of society rather than that of the criminal. The only time that the criminal is excluded from, therefore, is the one from which he is meant to be excluded: the time that passes in the social space.

IX. *Templum, Tempus*

Montesquieu notes that temples were shelters for criminals, especially in Greece, where killers, rejected from the city and the presence of men, had no other refuge but temples and no other guardians but the gods. He says, in reference to Tacitus: "it was difficult for magistrates to police, because the temple protected the crimes of men just as it protected the ceremonies of the gods."[53]

The temple allowed the criminal to survive. If imprisonment, as we have seen, is considered a relaxation of capital punishment, it is also, at the same time, a refuge. A temple served the same function as a modern prison: hiding a criminal, hiding him from sight. In Mosaic law involuntary killers were considered innocent but were kept out of sight of the victim's relatives. In accordance with Montesquieu we could suggest that just as the temple protects the sacred ceremony so the prison protects the criminal (although the object of protection would be not society, as often maintained, but rather the criminal himself).This analogy with the temple leads us to another, still more relevant to our subject matter. "Just as a church constitutes a break in the profane space of a modern city, the religious service that is celebrated within it points at a break in the profane temporal duration. "[54] Likewise in prison, just as there is a break in the space marked by the prison walls, so there is a rupture in time.

This intersection of time and space marks the beginning of a different type of duration, qualitatively distinct despite the punishment being measured out with the same unit as that used to measure social time, common time.

X. The Time of Punishment

The topic of the relationship between time and punishment, of the use of time as punishment, of time as something more than the measurement of punishment, leads us inevitably to the relationship between time and law. Punishment is one area in which law makes time conditional upon its own ends. One could also say that law assimilates the passage of a certain time, the time of the person subject to punishment, to a passage of time that is specific to law.

For Gerhart Husserl,[55] this passage of real time specific to law is not the natural flow and simple duration of instants. Law's time is rather an abstract time, precisely because it seeks to go beyond what is immediate and contingent in a naive experience of time.

The world of natural experience, the everyday world of human beings, is a world ruled by doubt. Human indigence consists precisely in the impossibility of controlling the future. The impossibility of foretelling the future originates in the transient nature of the human being, which in turn stems from his only certainty: his being is a being that flows towards death. When the law derives legal consequences from the social circumstances of real life, it excludes the fact that such real life flows towards an uncertain future. Given its inherent propensity for transcendence, the law tries to free itself from doubt and transience. Legal rules establish a world that knows nothing of doubt. In this world the future does not exist, in that it has already been anticipated by the rules.

Nevertheless, in order for the law to become a concrete reality, in order for it to be "realized," it must move from the "detemporalized" world it has created to the real social life that relates to the natural flow of time. It must return to the temporal dimension from which it has broken away. This process takes place through the application of legal rules.

"Objective time – says Gerhart Husserl – does not flow faster or slower depending on whether a child, an old man, a patient at the dentist's, a speaker at a public meeting, or a soldier on the battlefield is affected by the passing of time." One can say exactly the opposite, however, if the passing of time is experienced within someone's conscience. Thus, to natural time and to the abstract time of law we must add subjective time, the time of conscience.[56]

What happens with punishment? The legal ruling that establishes a punishment anticipates the future by determining a certain amount of time as the duration of punishment. The duration, however, will not be the mere succession of instants of natural time but an objective, abstract duration, measured irrespective of any concrete contents not relevant to its purpose. When punishment is applied to a person, it becomes "temporalized" in the lifetime of the subject. Time will follow the flow of natural time in the subject's biological life: it will follow his gradual aging and may even be interrupted by his death. In this case, objective time will preclude the fulfillment of the time period stipulated by the law.

However, the time of punishment is also experienced in the conscience of the subject living through it. Punishment has also a third temporal dimension: subjective time, the time of conscience. "If we understand what it means, for instance, really 'to live the time,' we realize that each person lives a common, shared time, that I too can understand, but lives also in a time entirely his own, untranslatable, a time each person feels for himself, in the same way that he alone experiences his hunger, lives his life, and dies his death.... No one can replace another in this experience, at once shared and individual."[57]

Here the non-substitutable nature of the experience of the person who lives the punishment is underscored. If "each person feels for himself," he will also live the punishment "for himself," as a unique, non-transferable experience. Although a punishment may have been decided upon and quantified in a uniform and objective manner, each person will experience it as his own. Each person will live his own unique punishment.

On the one hand, the same unit measures the time of punishment as it passes, even as the punishment itself takes shape in the passing of time. On the other hand, a perception of this passing time develops within the subject. On the one hand, magnitude; on the other, intensity. "If magnitude, outside you, is never intensive, then intensity, within you, is never magnitude."[58]

The quality of time lived during punishment, by virtue of being precisely the "time of punishment," cannot be the same as the quality of time lived free from punishment. Any activity that is carried out during such time will not be authentic; it will be infused with the time and space of punishment. Even though he might seem to be in motion, the subject of the punishment is moored to a specific space where a different time goes by. This immobility could be regarded as waiting. This waiting "involves the entire living being, suspends his activity and immobilizes him in the anxiety that it causes him." And even though it does not refer to the punishment, the following definition by Minkowski seems appropriate here: "in the waiting the being recoils, becomes encapsulated, tries – one could say – to expose as little of himself as possible to the aggressions of a hostile environment, and, acting this way, detaches himself from this environment, draws his own boundaries against it."[59] This recoiling, this drawing of boundaries against a hostile environment, is an indication of the subject's internal isolation, resulting from the external isolation that punishment, as a form of expulsion, has imposed on him.

"The other," which arouses in him a memory of himself, has been left outside the prison walls. Those who share the convict's fate cannot awaken in him a "memory of himself," the memory of who he used to be before the onset of punishment, but can only remind him of his actual state. This is why the relationships he develops in prison do not help him to recall himself or to know again who he was before his time and space were severed by punishment. His ability to remember will be limited and impaired because his memory has been left to its own devices: it is no longer receiving the external stimulation of the world, that world which used to be his but which has now shut its doors on him.

Relationships of coexistence that develop within the prison walls can therefore never be free, since they have been imposed by the circumstances of punishment. They are relationships among those excluded from the community. This exclusion can then include them in another community, one based upon a common wait: the wait for its own dissolution.

If these are the conditions peculiar to those living through punishment, then their times should be the present of the past and the present of the future, which correspond to memory and to waiting, respectively: "Perhaps it would be exact to say: there are three times: a present of things past, a present of things present, and a present of things to come. In the soul there are these three aspects of time, and I do not see them anywhere else."[60]

In punishment, the vision of the present is blurred by the expectation of the future. The present has worth only as a path to the future since, as we have seen, the entire being is focused upon waiting.

As in the verse referred to by Saint Augustine, punishment, before it begins, is pure expectation, but as it follows its course it passes into memory. The present of the punishment forms only a passage from what is expected to what is remembered. Since punishment is an injury, the entire being will try to avoid it by turning to memory or expectation. The present will then be pure simultaneity, the intersection of time and prison, which is the space of punishment.

XI. Conclusion

The problem of the just proportion between crime and punishment is obscured by the non-retributive purposes assigned to imprisonment.

As Mathieu points out, imprisonment has, in effect, become practically the only means by which to punish a crime, but not because of an appreciation of its symbolic value or any attempt to suppress the criminal's will. The main reason, according to Mathieu, is different: punishment has been understood as a means of defense for society and its members; holding the culprit in prison keeps him from causing harm. It is precisely because imprisonment has become the only modality of punishment that there is an attempt to justify punishment by justifying imprisonment.[61]

Aside from this justification of imprisonment as a safety measure, it is also argued that imprisonment is only a means to correct or reform a criminal. It is supposed to be a service provided by the community to those of its members who, through their actions, have shown that they need to undergo corrective therapy. This analogy between the role of the judge and that of the doctor, between punishment and therapy, crime and the symptoms of an illness, recurs often in Plato's dialogues.[62]

Both in the case of imprisonment as a safety measure and in the case of imprisonment as amendment or cure, the problem arises as to how to establish its duration, for duration, as we have seen, is the fundamental element in punishment by imprisonment.

When will there be complete certainty that the subject no longer represents a danger to the community? How can that moment be determined in advance? This question could form the link between the two theories, since its answer might be, once they have made amends. But how to examine the criminal so as to be certain of his reform? One answer would be to look for outward signs of such a transformation. But who would be qualified to interpret such signs? If the individual concerned was assumed to be ill, then a physician or psychologist might possibly be appropriate; if he was assumed to be a social misfit, then he might rather need a social worker. But then the role of the judge would be assumed by such professionals, and the execution of the sentence would be in their hands.[63] In such a case the sentence would not be a sentence so much as a prescription for treatment. And it would be very difficult to prescribe the length of the treatment beforehand and without a thorough knowledge of the patient. This problem would introduce a degree of uncertainty into law that law itself has always attempted to avoid, an uncertainty that would extend not only to the duration but also to the role of punishment, since the reform of a criminal would be as difficult to predict as the healing of someone sick. Punishment would thus be an institution of hypothetical, possible functions; it would be like establishing a legislative body not to pass laws, as such, but rather for the possibility that one day, no matter how remote, it might finally succeed in doing so.

In addition to this, the best evidence a criminal could give us of his good health would be his ability to lead a respectful life among others at the very heart of the community from which he had been removed. This would double the uncertainty: how long would he have to be under "surveillance" until he could be considered truly "healed"? And, on the other hand, recalling the security dimension attributed to his imprisonment, would the community be willing to run the risk of taking him back without irrefutable evidence of his harmlessness?

These considerations are not taken into account, however, when trying to establish the duration of punishment. It is all worked out in the simplest manner: the extent of the punishment is established in proportion to the crime. The objectives allegedly justifying punishment are not taken into account, but only the need for retribution according to the seriousness of the crime.

Obviously it makes no sense to establish the length of punishment on the basis of the seriousness of the crime when punishment is not punishment but rather therapy, correction, or a security measure. Correcting or curing someone who had committed murder would clearly not be the same as correcting or curing someone who had committed simple theft. And yet the latter person might turn out to be more "ill" or potentially dangerous than the former.

This contradiction between the extent of a punishment and the purpose attributed to it stems from the need to offer guaranties to the subject of punishment. I see the fundamental problem as the following: punishment, even if considered a security measure or therapy, remains punishment nevertheless.

First, both are imposed upon the individual concerned regardless of his own will. And second, not only are they in most cases experienced as punishments, but also, objectively, from a social perspective, they are considered nasty consequences of reprehensible acts. Thus, punishment is inflicted even when unacknowledged.

As Mathieu observes, the mistake is to some extent intentional: one wants to continue to punish while at the same time denying that one does so. Society, through the judge, finds an excuse to subject the convict to a suffering that "has every appearance of a punishment," although punishment – and this is made clear – it is not.[64]

This reasoning leads us to infer that punishment may be applied "unintentionally," even if it is then deprived of one of its essential features: measure, in the sense of moderation, or *modus* insofar as it means reflection, deliberation. What we might call the "planning" of punishment would therefore be missing in imprisonment viewed as security measure or therapy. The inflicted injury would be collateral, incidental.

Given the need to protect the subject against a "measureless" ill by adjusting it to a pre-established measure, there are in this regard plenty of reasons to justify the logic of retribution. Following this logic, a punishment would always be established in relation to the past, to the criminal act. The measure of punishment would thus have, as far as possible, a clearer and more precise benchmark than that provided by a prospective cure or rehabilitation, which would be uncertain and lacking a specific timeline.

Retributive logic is based, furthermore, upon a notion of "dignity" which cannot properly be applied to someone undergoing correction or therapy,[65] a process that would, rather, be attributable to a child or madman. Naturally this requires a definition of "dignity" that, in this particular context, would appear to denote a certain capacity to commit criminal offences.

Prison, the site *par excellence* of the application of punishment, can be defined by one single characteristic: it is, as has already been indicated, located beyond social space. Punishment by imprisonment is therefore assignment to a place outside social space. Punishment by imprisonment is the exclusion from social space. This is the primary goal of imprisonment: exclusion. Any future participation in the community and in the community's space requires this prior exclusion.

The link between crime and punishment, furthermore, is clear – both are injuries. From this perspective, whoever disrupts the symmetry of social communication must then be deprived of the social communication that he has disrupted. But "the crime has a definite qualitative and quantitative reach, its negation should be similarly definite."[66]

The problem lies precisely in comparing "the qualitative and quantitative reach" of crime and punishment. For crime and punishment, quite simply, are heterogeneous; but according to their value, to their general attribute of being injuries, they are comparable. It is up to the intellect to find an approximation of value equivalence between them.[67]

Yet how might the intellect compare the injury that makes a crime with the quantitative and abstract temporal determination of punishment by imprisonment?

What relationship endures between the duration of the punishment and the seriousness of the crime? If the seriousness of the crime is its intensity, how to determine the intensity of the punishment? What time-scale would correspond to such intensity? Is it possible to measure the intensity of punishment on the basis of objective time, using the same units in which working time and social time are measured? And if it were possible, how many units of time would correspond to each crime?

It is not possible, however, given that quantitative and abstract temporal determination, by itself, lacks punitive content. How can a number, so many months, so many years, so many days, be turned into intensity? Such a conversion from quantity into intensity can take place only within the subject's own conscience, because intensity is an inner, personal, intimate, and non-transferable phenomenon. Each person lives his punishment in a unique and unpredictable way. Therefore, when a sentence is passed, one cannot know for certain the punishment that is being applied. The time units used to determine a punishment will follow one another at a greater or lesser speed depending on the subject. And only as he internalizes this duration will the punishment take shape.

In prison, the execution of punishment is entrusted to time. A subject, expelled from the community, who enters prison will not be the same when he leaves and rejoins the community from which he was expelled. Time (irrespective of the conditions of its passing) will work this gradual transformation. However peculiar it might be, the time of punishment has in common with time in liberty the fact that it is always the time of a human being's life. The years of punishment go by, and so do those of life.

As Agustin said, do the years in a lifetime increase or decrease? When does the road end? It does not end at the same time for everyone. Each person comes to the end of the road at his own time. This life is the road; once you come to the end of your life, you have come to the end of the road. We walk, and as we live, we move forward. Can you imagine remaining in the same place while time passes by? It is impossible. Time walks forward and we walk along with it, and instead of increasing, the years of our lifetime decrease.... Our years come, you have said, but I will show you that rather than coming, they leave. You will see how simply I can demonstrate this. Let us suppose we know how many years this boy will live. Let us be generous, say eighty. He will live to be an old man. Write down eighty. He has lived one already. How many have you counted? How old was he? Eighty. Take one off. He has lived ten already? There are seventy left. Has he lived twenty already? He has sixty years left. True, the years were growing, but what kind of growth is that? Our years come and go. They are not here to remain with us. They run us over; they step on us and make us worthy of less and less, day after day.[68]

Chapter Two

Piranesi: Space, Time, and Punishment

The feeling that Piranesi's *Carceri* arouses in the spectator is a combination of horror and bewilderment. Bewilderment before a space that cannot be comprehended, reached, or measured; horror at the possibility of being forced to wander about this space, of being thrown into it. Horror can also be linked to the *sublime*, which unites the horrible with the magnificent, "*il Basso e l'Alto*" of the human spirit. Precisely, the *Carceri* do not follow the dictums of classical beauty or baroque wonder but rather the romantic rules of the sublime. "All buildings intended to awaken the idea of the sublime should be dark and gloomy."[69]

It is also possible to associate the vast dimensions of Piranesi's *Carceri* with a sense of profound emptiness, loneliness, and silence: in one word, a sense of absence.

In addition, the interplay of images and sensations that they awaken evokes a notion of pain that is engendered, in its full scale of anxiety and torment, by the notion of the sublime. All these representations of emptiness and anxiety, which fill our spirit with horror but at the same time lift it by sublimating that same horror, cannot be denied the attributes of a nightmare, of a dream.[70]

However, the *Carceri* do not belong to the dream world. They are not mere vertigos of imagination, unconnected to real meanings or references.[71] They are not simply dreams or delirium. Rather, they are the product of a reflection embodied in an image-idea: the idea of the superiority of the Roman *lex* and its justice. They reaffirm the thought expressed by Piranesi in his work *Della Magnificenza ed Architettura dei Romani*, where he claims the autonomy and priority of Roman law vis-a-vis Greek law.[72]

Piranesi reflects the culture of the Enlightenment, for the dreamlike vision of the *Carceri* is not valued as an end in itself, but rather as something that is ideologically oriented towards an invention that it evokes and celebrates at the same time. It is a fantastic visit, as in a dream, to the ancient Roman jail and, on a symbolic level, to the exemplary Roman *lex*.[73]

Therefore, one can infer that the discourse expressed by the *Carceri* is a legal discourse, not only because they exalt the Roman *lex*, but also because they are designed to kindle a certain feeling in the spectator: the feeling of terror in the face of the application of law consolidated in the walls of those prisons and sublimated in their dark and abyssal rooms. (*Ad terrorem increscentis audaciae* can be read on *Tavola XVI*.) Their goal is to put an end to growing crime. They try to exemplify what would happen to those who dare to violate the *lex*.

That message, however, like any message, entails the existence of a recipient capable of understanding it. It presupposes the watchful and alert presence of a subject that understands the language expressed by the image. It presupposes the existence of a community that communicates, that is, a group of people that can immediately comprehend the message conveyed by the image.

For that to be possible, an implicit general meaning must exist, a rationality that makes up the *ethos* of that community: a feeling of worthiness that coincides with the feeling of belonging to a community that imposes its rules on us in order to exist. It is the feeling that opens up the very possibility of community life.

As a response to crime, imprisonment is a readily comprehensible element of legal discourse. Its first, manifest, and undisputed role is to separate. This, in turn, directly affects the feeling of belonging to a community, since it causes an exclusion from it. In this sense, it has a deep retributive character: a breach of the rules that make possible the existence of the community presupposes an intentional separation from it, and the breach is punished with a forced separation from it. That is, he who acts against the existence of the community or puts it in jeopardy is consequently separated from the common coexistence.

But the exclusive reaction of punishment is also an exemplary reaction. It works as an example: an example of what happens in a given case, to predict what would happen in a similar case. If a crime was left unpunished, one could infer that a similar crime could also be left unpunished. Imprisonment not only inflicts exclusion as a form of retribution for a certain crime, it also attempts to persuade with an example that it will react in a similar way to a similar crime.

Nevertheless, one does not go directly from one particular case to another. The example is an element in the process of theoretical induction: one proceeds from particular to particular through the implicit loop of the general. A class of reactions is inferred from an object, and a new object is deduced from the class. In the legal discourse, the rule is the implicit loop of the general, the link between particular cases. The legal rule imparts a persuasive message; however, it does not attempt to persuade a single individual, but all individuals. In fact, its real recipient is the very community that has created it. It is a discourse in which the sender is identical to the addressee.

Piranesi's *Carceri* translate the dialectics of the legal message into images. They unfold as a sort of spectacle to be seen from the city. From the top of bridges and arches, citizens can see prisoners roaming about the prison. In other words, in these prisons punishment is not secretly carried out.[74] In some of the *Tavole* there even seems to be a continuum between jail space and city space (particularly in *Tavole V*, added for the second edition, where, though in the background, one can clearly see a stairway, a building, and the sky).

The "visibility" of the *Carceri* also corresponds to the contents of the message conveyed by punishment. It persuades not only by constituting a warning but also by relaying an attitude of disapproval that the community assumes against crime.

Alessandro Baratta agrees with this interpretation. Referring to positive general prevention theories, he states that "the message implied by criminal law or by the perception of the punishment inflicted on criminals, is invested [by these theories] with the function of expressing and asserting values and rules, thus contributing to their validity and to a social integration centred on these values and rules, as to rebuilding institutional confidence in those rules that have been broken by the impingement."[75]

Punishment, established and applied by the community, expresses and conveys a message from the community to the community. Hence the clarity of Piranesi's gloomy *Carceri*: their grandeur expresses the magnificence of the law, the violation of which they punish. At the same time, they present themselves, in their monumental appearance, as the work of a collective, eternal subject. And they are addressed to a subject that is worthy of receiving their message and that is also collective and eternal. Piranesi enlarges, magnifies, and amplifies all the space and monuments he reproduces. That is why what probably most strikes at first sight is the *Carceri's* only slight resemblance to the traditional image of a jail. The nightmare of imprisonment has always consisted of being enclosed in a narrow space: "Tu, in questa tomba ... " In the *Carceri*, on the contrary, the space of constriction is almost infinite.

In the *Carceri*, the condition of segregation, of separation, is brought about not by walls or by the firmness of bars or by the lack of communication with the outside but by the impossibility of finding in them a space that could be seen to fit human beings. (M. Yourcenar observes that plants and animals have been excluded from them).

The exorbitant magnitudes and the sheer vastness of spaces in Piranesi can be appreciated only by comparison with the human figure. We notice the true dimension of the walls when we compare them with the tiny human figures that roam within them. It is evident that the prison is too big for them. They do not belong there. A human being is too small to move along such boundless space, to embrace such pillars. The monumental character of the *Carceri* is further heightened if perceived in relation to the human figure.

As we have seen, for Piranesi the distortion of real proportions does not pursue an aesthetic goal. The places and monuments devised by him are not just recollections but models designed to help in the construction of an ideal society. Their value is not nostalgic; it is philosophical, moral, political, and legal.[76]"Raised to the dimension of the gigantic, supporting an aesthetic and ethical dream, [Piranesi] confirms that there are no preconceived forms to the spirit's visions."[77] In other words, for the spiritual, moral, and ethical dimension of his discourse, of the discourse expressed by his images, there are no pre-established structures. Everything is valid as long as it fulfils its expressive role. That is why the figures imprisoned in the *Carceri* do not belong in the *Carceri*: these have not been conceived for them. They are destined not for the man of flesh and bones but for all men; they are designed to stop not just one man's boldness but every man's boldness. One must not forget that a prison is a locus of punishment. And without the presence of the community, punishment is no longer punishment. It is not by chance that theories that legitimate the purposes of punishment have always given more consideration to the effects it can have on society than to those it can produce on the individual.

The *Carceri* not only emphasize the lack of proportion that has always existed between the human figure and the monument;

they also express a coincidence between a prison and monument. Piranesi has created a prison monument or a monumental prison. A common feature connects both concepts: duration. Both share a vocation: permanence, stability, and persistence in time and in spite of time. Nothing is more opposed to the notion of monument than the ephemeral. And nothing is more contrary to the purpose of prison than the lack of duration that is implied by the ephemeral.

When arguing in favour of punishment by imprisonment, Beccaria singles out the lasting impression it causes in men's spirits as its most important feature. And he stresses, "It is not the severity of punishment that has the greatest impact on the human mind, but rather its duration."[78] Likewise, when he sees imprisonment as opposed to capital punishment, he points once again to duration as an advantage of prison: "The most powerful restraint against crime is not the terrible but fleeting spectacle of a villain's death, but the faint and prolonged example of a man who, deprived of his liberty, has become a beast of burden, repaying the society he has offended with his labors."[79]

His stance, manifestly utilitarian, does not ascribe a retributive purpose to duration but rather a dissuasive one. Duration is important insofar as it impresses the message of the punishment upon the minds it is addressed to. The duration, according to Beccaria's explications, is addressed not to the offender but to the community that observes his punishment. Beccaria would build prisons that would be similar to Piranesi's, since the public, the community, should be able to see what goes on inside them. Not only would Beccaria's jails be open to the exterior, they would also be monumental, because they would have to address the entire community.

Punishment represents the community's disapproval of crime; it makes it clear that the community and crime do not go together. Even though the victim may be an individual, the community assumes the damage caused by crime as its own, taking on the role of the fundamental victim.[80] For that reason, Beccaria declares that the true measure of crime, of its seriousness, is the harm done to the entire society.[81] The seriousness of a crime is an essential element in the logic of punishment, and punishment, as opposed to any spontaneous, violent, and simply vindictive reaction, also has a measure, which corresponds to the measure of crime. Severity of punishment and seriousness of crime? There should be so close a correspondence between the two that, according to Beccaria, "If geometry were adaptable to the infinite and obscure arrangements of human activity, there ought to be a corresponding scale of punishments, descending from the most rigorous to the slightest."[82]

Geometry, however, cannot be adapted to human actions, precisely because they present themselves in obscure and infinite combinations. Nothing is more opposed to geometric rigor than human activity. Hence the perennial dissatisfaction that the measuring of punishments carries with it. It seems that accuracy is sought precisely where it cannot be found. All the calculations are made, but the outcome is absurd. The ideal proportion is never found.

The same happens with Piranesi's *Carceri*. The lack of correspondence between them and their prisoners, and the disproportionate magnitude of the walls in relation to the human figure are not a consequence of a lack of calculations: "The vertigo we feel before the irrational world of the *Carceri* is not due to a lack of measurements (we know Piranesi was not much of a geometrician) but rather to multifarious calculations which we know to be accurate and which, nevertheless, lead to proportions that we know to be false."[83]

Just as the *Carceri* do not correspond with the human figure, neither does the duration of imprisonment coincide with the duration of human life.

The prison as perceived in our day-to-day lives is a building, not a monument. Its dimensions respond, or try to respond, to a specific function: locking in a certain number of people. However, in the city this building is not just one among many. It is the "locus of punishment." The monumental dimension attributed to it has nothing to do with the organization of space but with that of time. The extent of the community's disapproval is expressed not so much in the construction of the prison as in the establishment of the duration of the punishment.

In the *Carceri*, the passing of the time of punishment is shaped, embodied, carved in the exorbitance of the walls, in the firmness of the bars, in the somber tonality pervading them. As M. Yourcenar says, this playing with space is equivalent to that devised in the work of a brilliant novelist by virtue of the liberties taken with time. When fixing the punishment of imprisonment, the legal system works as a novelist, taking liberties with the time of the subject of law.

The legislator has conceived law to be characterized by stability, eternity, and strength. The mere fact of a punishment being fixed that may exceed the life possibilities of a human being shows that the subject of the punishment "enjoys" a special time, a time that is not contingent upon the scarcity characterizing the time of the man of flesh and bones. Prison therefore provides the subject with stability in time as well as space. It endows him with an object-like quality, "precisely because stability is what characterizes that which, within the historic horizon of the destiny of being, is given as being, as thing, as object."[84] This "objectification" of the subject of law, through the stability granted to it when punishment is applied, clearly coincides with its use as the vehicle of a message addressed to everyone.

The legal system, in order to fulfill its duty, namely to persuade, influence, and guide human behavior, needs to create a universe of its own. This universe does not reflect the real universe in the way of a descriptive science. The law is interested in real life insofar as it wishes to modify it or to prevent it from being modified – insofar as it is determined to influence it.

Thus, in this universe of legal thought the subject created by this thought has features that have no correlation with those of a mortal subject. For punishment and the measuring out of punishment have been conceived only with regard to the target of the message: the community. The individual is nothing more than the means by which this message is transmitted. The tiny beings that roam about the *Carceri* possess little reality, little humanity. As M. Yourcenar observes, the true horror of the prisons lies not so much in mysterious scenes of torture as in the indifferent attitude of the human ants that wander around those immense spaces … and the most extraordinary feature of this disquieting miniature crowd is their immunity to vertigo. Apparently they are unaware even of the fact that they are standing at the edge of an abyss.[85]

Again we find in Piranesi the concepts that, when translated into visual images, constitute the essence of the punishment of imprisonment. Just as Piranesi's creatures seem invulnerable to a fall in space, the creature of the legal system seems invulnerable to the fall entailed by the passing of time. It would seem that the law has itself conceived both the time of the punishment and the subject that does that time, taking no notice of real living conditions.

The prison designed by Piranesi is also a world within a world. If, as we observe its minute creatures, our feeling is that they inhabit a space that does not correspond to them, so the prisoner makes us feel that the time of his punishment does not correspond to him either.

There is no correlation because it forms part of a discourse addressed to the community, and the community determines the duration of punishment with regard to its own time, not that of the subject, which is merely a vehicle of its message.

"How narrowly bounded is our lifetime, we see and count the number of our years. But have the years of nations been seen by mortal eye?"[86]This is why the legal system is so generous with the time of punishment – because it is a time that belongs to the community. The community, as a collective and anonymous being, always has time because it never dies. And it never dies because death is in every case my death, your death.[87] The community knows only of public time, which, being uniform and even, belongs to everyone, and therefore, to no one. Such is the time that is measured when establishing the duration of a punishment. It is measured with an immutable unit so that everyone can "reckon" on it simultaneously.[88] This time, of which, after being measured, nothing is to be found except a number and a stretch,[89] is social time, the time that passes in our daily life. The same daily life into which we have incorporated the prison as one more building among the many that surround us. A building that conceals its true character: that of a monument and, as such, a symbol.

In contrast to the *Carceri*, with which Piranesi wishes to intimidate us, we have built prisons that facilitate indifference and forgetfulness, these being the true pillars on which our punishments rest. Just as Piranesi's perspectives induce a specific appreciation of their dimensions, the separation and remoteness of those who dwell in our prisons keep us from truly appraising the intensity of their punishment. "Does it happen only to eyesight that seeing objects from afar or close by distorts the truth and causes false judgments? Or does not the same thing happen also in the case of pleasure and pain?"[90] Therefore, one should inquire to what extent punishment does indeed convey its persuasive message; to what extent it accomplishes a dissuasive function; to what extent it is worth imposing.

Piranesi's *Carceri* do not so much conceal as bring out the exorbitance, the "overabundance," of punishment. In our prisons these attributes are linked not to space but to time. Just as it seems that upon entering the *Carceri*, Piranesi's figurines lose their real dimension, so flesh-and-blood men, upon entering the space of imprisonment, lose their true temporal dimension. The proportion between the time measured by punishment, public time, and individual time, which corresponds to the life of the subject of punishment, is the same that exists between the walls and the arches of the *Carceri* and the human figures that roam about within them. Just as the *Carceri* are "too large" to fit the prisoners, so the collective time that measures punishment is "too large" to fit the individual.

The law, however, pays no attention to this disproportion; it has created its own universe in order to convey its discourse of persuasion. And within this universe, it uses and measures time to meet its own ends. Perhaps the creation of a universe of its own on the part of the law reflects not an attitude of superiority but, on the contrary, a recognition of its own powerlessness. In other words, it reflects not an excessive optimism but rather an irreparable pessimism. "Legal thought also contains a pessimistic ingredient, based upon the assumption that complex phenomena cannot be comprehended thoroughly, that human actions cannot be foreseen, and that the infinite richness of reality cannot be systematized."[91]

Nevertheless, the fact that the law chooses to exclude death from the life of the subject of imprisonment does not prevent the individual who is the real life match of that subject of the legal universe from dying. He dies during the course of the punishment or he dies after the punishment, but he dies. If death is not factored into the legal calculation of punishment, then that calculation can lead to false proportions. Just as a man must never forget that he will die, because "this thought is the very palpitation of [his] consciousness,"[92] so the law must not address a weak and mortal subject as though he were neither weak nor mortal. Otherwise it will never achieve the fair equilibrium it seeks. In order to find this equilibrium, it may have to give up scientific calculations and claims that assist it in constructing an impoverished and distorted image of reality. "It is true that we regard, cultivate, and promote criminology as a science, but also as an art. We are aware that our knowledge can flow, advance by way of discourse, and/or through intuition. Multiple nuances mediate between one and the other. The discursive method proceeds by inducing and/or deducing one truth from another. In contrast the intuitive method knows the truth right away."[93] Intuition would never have allowed us to forget death. The individual, the man of flesh and bone, exists only between his birth and his death. In contrast to the community, he has only a limited amount of time available to him. In fact, all he really owns in this world is this stretch of time. Punishment by imprisonment, introduced to humanize the law, to replace the barbarity of corporal punishments, affects the subject at his most vulnerable point: the little time that he is allotted that constitutes his life.

The constant dissatisfaction in the search for a just proportion between crime and punishment results from a conception of a subject/prison inmate that follows not individual time, the time between birth and death, but collective time. Only when the legal system recognizes the mortality of its creature, the "temporality" which is his own, will it come somewhat closer to the equilibrium it seeks. Perhaps then it will recognize the true intensity of the punishment it applies. Prison will then reveal its real dimensions, just as Piranesi has unfolded them in his most terrible *Carceri.*

Chapter Three

The Victim and the Non-subject of Law

In an article entitled "Sur les traces du non-sujet de droit,"[94] Jean Carbonnier offers an example that set me thinking: a survey of the relationship established between taxi drivers and their clients indicates that the former complain about being totally ignored by the latter, who act as if they were not present. In short, they complain about being "non-persons."Carbonnier observes that specialists in victimology would interpret such complaints by arguing that perhaps the drivers unconsciously hope for the gunshot that would then promote them to the status of persons. I believe, however, that specialists in victimology would also question whether the driver, by becoming a victim, would genuinely secure for himself a leading role or even simply a less marginal one. For what usually occurs is exactly the opposite. Whereas the client, from the moment he aims the gun at the driver and turns him into his victim, is giving him an importance he has not given him before, the same cannot be said of the penal system.

The evolution of criminal law is characterized by a shift of focus away from the victim and towards the author of the crime. "Progressively, as the State began to take on responsibility for the administration of justice, the criminal became the main character in law courts, relegating the victim to a secondary role to the point, later on, of being almost completely forgotten."[95] The "specificity" of the criminal law approach vis-à-vis that of other legal disciplines consists precisely in this "removal" of the victim.[96] Working from this premise, the victim is easily incorporated into the category of "non-subject of law" developed by Carbonnier to shed light upon the category of the subject of law. Regarding the latter he indicates that, more than a receptacle of acquired rights, the law is the issuer and receiver of legal acts and facts. The subject of law is, before anything else, a subject, an owner of actions before justice. And he adds: "Perhaps the most authentic subjects of law are found gripping a spear."

The merit attributed to the penal system is precisely that it has taken the spear "from the grip" of the victim, thus preventing eventual revenge. By taking away the spear, however, other faculties that would have given the victim importance in the criminal and judicial systems are likewise taken away.

How can the "non-subject of law" be characterized? It is difficult to define a negative concept. Carbonnier suggests that the non-subject of law becomes aware of his plight under the sting of pain, since a previous condition had allowed him to experience the status of subject of law. Thus, according to this reasoning, the non-subject of law is a former subject of law, someone who has lost, or has been demoted from, his status as subject of law. He is someone stripped of something. The victim, in particular, has been dispossessed by the criminal system, which has deprived the true victim of his status as victim, in order to bestow this status upon the community. The penal system has replaced the real and concrete victim with a symbolic and abstract victim: the community.

Just as in some systems the responsibility of the individual is extended to the group, so in the modern criminal system the "victimization" of the individual is extended to the institutionalized community. This substitution, however, does not imply an increasing concern for collective victims, minorities, ethnic groups, or oppressed peoples. In other words, it does not imply substituting the collective individual for the single individual. The substitution taking place is that of an abstract entity, the community, for a flesh-and-blood individual or group. And any abstract entity involves mental effort, involves imagination. The personification of the community and of the State is the fruit of a specific sort of legal thought that, in turn, is a product of rationalism. whose fundamental process is the conquering of the world as "conceived image."[97] On the one hand, man represents himself as a subject; on the other, he represents the world as image: an interrelation that is critical to the essence of modernity. Once he has conceived of himself as a subject that represents the world, he is able not only to conceive of the world in a certain way but also to represent himself to himself in any particular manner he may choose. In this way the legislator was able to elaborate a legal subject having no grounds in reality whatsoever. The entire legal universe is a product of reason. If the accepted parameters are applied to this universe, anything goes, even replacing the flesh-and-blood victim by the victim conceived of by the legal system.

It is not mere chance that this substitution has taken place at a specific historical moment. Never before has the non-individual been so important under the form of the collective.[98] The law is becoming less and less interested in the individual as such. We are witnessing a process of "de-individualization of the individual." There is no place within the law for the fate of pure individuality. The fate of the individual acquires shape and meaning only insofar as he forms part of a higher order, such as society, history, and the species.[99] A higher order of abstraction, we should add. In this connection, P. Barcellona points out the contradictory structure of modern subjectivity: its starting point is an individualistic anthropology associated with private property and economic free enterprise which develops on the basis of a radical individualism but which, at the same time, necessitates a universal capable of combining within itself a multiplicity of individuals at a level that allows for the individual to be conceived of within the framework of a general order of social living. This is the level of abstraction of monetary and legal relationships. The subject of law, along with the consequent possible existence of the "non-subject of law," is precisely the bridging-category, the junction-category, that makes possible the coexistence of radical individualism and the general order – the abstract, legal order – of social living. The subject is not the individual: the individual is pure fact; but the subject is a product of the legal system.[100]

In the symbolic universe of law, it is equally valid to confer the value of subject of law upon an abstract entity, produced by a specific conception, as it is to assign it to an individual, a man of flesh and blood. And akin to the notion of the community as subject of the law-victim, there is a corresponding notion, no less abstract or imaginary: the notion of the subject of the law/author of the crime. Some traits of omnipotence are attributed to him insofar as he is considered capable of resisting internal, as well as external, conditioning; likewise of being immortal, as shown by the duration of some punishments which go well beyond any human being's reasonable life expectancy. And this immortality is correlative to that of the abstract victim created by the criminal system: the community.

The community, by virtue of the legal system, takes ownership of the damage caused by crime. The crime is measured in relation to the community and its time: "We have seen what the true measure of crimes is – namely, *the harm done to society.*"[101] The duration of the punishment is measured on the basis of social and not individual time. We might ask, however, how the time of one can be measured out in punishment by taking into account the time belonging to the other? It seems impossible to establish an adequate proportion. And so the frustration generated by this powerlessness in relation to measuring out punishment is what underlies the "bad conscience" that has given rise to attending to the recipient of this unsatisfactory measure. "The penal model ..., ever since the victim disappeared as a consequence of the expropriation of the conflict by the sovereign or the State, has ceased to be a model for solving conflict, because of the elimination of one of the parties to the conflict. This accounts for the unbelievable proliferation of theories of punishment (and consequent theories of criminal law) and for the wandering philosophical pilgrimage of criminal knowledge."[102]

The passage just quoted amounts to saying that the approach to the problem must be turned on its head: it is not the focus on the offender and the punishment that causes the displacement of the victim, but rather the opposite. As the individual-victim is replaced by the community-victim and as the victim is thereby relegated to the background, the real terms of the conflict are deeply altered. And the response to the crime is altered accordingly. Owing to the lack of adequate proportion between the crime and the response to the crime, the recipient of such an inadequate proportion becomes the main focus; he becomes, in turn, a "victim" of the penal system. And criminal law takes care of its own possible victim.

The community considers itself the victim of an injury that is defined as evil and not as suffering, because suffering is an individual experience. An evil does not always involve suffering. It is a breach of the rules, an unlawfulness, an alteration of the system's equilibrium: it belongs to the symbolic realm of the law. In this regard, another interpretation of the causes that have led to the displacement of the victim could also be suggested. The emphasis placed on the recipient of the punishment reveals, on a moral level, that the punishment prevails over the reparation of the injury caused by the crime. Injury equals evil; punishment equals suffering. Luigi Pareyson points out the positive value that has been attributed to suffering. It has been claimed that when evil is followed by suffering, there is no increased negativity, no doubling or proliferation of evil, but rather its cancellation. The "algebra of suffering" comes into play: minus times minus = more; negative times negative = positive.[103] This author's explanation is given in a context in which suffering acquires the redeeming value of atonement; but insofar as the recipient of the punishment accepts, seeks, and desires the suffering, I believe that this "algebra of suffering," which regards punishment as the most significant moment, constitutes the very basis of criminal law. The destruction of evil is, at the same time, the establishment of good. Denouncing evil is the equivalent of affirming the good.[104] This perspective, which has deep religious roots, has influenced our entire penal system and lies at its foundations. The positive value assigned to suffering is the helm that guides the ship – a suffering that is not regarded as evil, because it makes possible the elimination of evil. And if suffering itself is not regarded as evil, then neither will the victim's suffering be regarded as such. Therefore, reparation for such suffering will be given secondary importance. If suffering has a positive value, then the victim, the "subject" of such suffering, does not deserve the primary attention of penal law, which is, as its name implies, concerned with punishment. In short, according to this interpretation, criminal law is interested not in eliminating suffering but rather in eliminating evil (the description of which is found in the different statutory definitions of criminal acts). And so great is the concern with the elimination of evil, which is represented by the damage resulting from crime, that the victim's suffering is displaced, or even forgotten.

Nevertheless, over time a growing sensitivity in the face of suffering has been steadily developing, displaying, among other things, a concern for discovering the individual behind the mask which has been assigned to him in the conception of the image of the world. As the subject of law is more and more "fleshed out" into a real-life individual, the suffering he may experience may also awaken a sensitivity previously stifled by other considerations. Only by incorporating the individual will the law give to suffering its due importance, for suffering is a deeply individual experience. And the more it becomes interested in individual suffering the more it will become interested in the victims of crime and in the means by which to prevent their own suffering.

Returning to the work of Jean Carbonnier, from where we began, it seems as if there has existed in law a force that has opposed the creation of non-subjects: "Just [like]a spring that is compressed for an instant, the non-subject tends inevitably to become subject once again. Laws defer to this force." He provides several examples of this force, referring to cases such as those of slaves and foreigners. We could add victims, as well. Little by little, victimology has managed to incorporate victims not only into criminal legal discourse but also into penal and procedural legislation.

In another volume[105] Carbonnier himself refers to this trend: "Nevertheless, criminal law today does not limit itself to repairing its own deficiencies. One of its most outstanding successes has been to mobilize victims, to reverse their role," turning them from passive subjects of crime into active subjects that assert their own right to reparation. This trend, which runs parallel to a more humane vision of the offender and the punishment, reflects an attempt to recover the flesh-and-blood human being, whether victim or culprit. It is necessary to set aside artificial legal contrivance and to go straight to the reality that the law purports to address: man. As stated by Carbonnier, "better than subject of law, one should say: human being."

The presence of the human being in legal thought would bring about many radical changes and a different way of viewing things; above all, it would bring an end to the existence of non-subjects of law. As Carbonnier describes them in his concluding remarks: "their footprints are light and will soon be effaced from the sands of law."

Chapter Four

The Hermeneutic Circles of Punishment

Quell'è'l più basso loco è'l più oscuro,
E'l più lontan dal ciel che tutto gira ...

— *Dante*

Penal law and human rights. If we leave out the nouns, singular in one case, plural in the other, the two adjectives are left face to face: "penal" and "human." "Penal" is associated with punishment, "human" with man, with human beings. Punishment is on one side, human beings on the other. We must not forget, however, that both adjectives modify nouns: "law" and "rights" respectively. In a strict, literal sense, penal law is the law that applies punishment to human beings. And human rights are above all the rights of human beings not to suffer punishment. There is also a distinction between the singular form of "penal law" and the plural form of "human rights." The former is the Law, one, a manifestation of the power of the State; the latter are rights, and they are multiple with regard not only to their number but also to their possessors.

It seems strange to refer to punishments provided for by penal law as violations of human rights, however. Given certain legal, political, and institutional conditions, criminal law has the legitimate power to establish punishments, just as it had the power, until a certain time, to punish by means of the most terrifying forms of torture that today we would not hesitate to describe as violations of human rights. Foucault reminds us that in the second half of the eighteenth century an almost unanimous opposition to torture developed. Such protest was expressed "as a cry from the heart or from an outraged nature"; even in the case of the most heinous of murderers, one thing at least had to be respected: his "humanity."[106]

"Humanity" was thus erected as a limit to punishment. Nevertheless, one can still wonder: what was the situation before the reaction against torture? Did those subjected to torture not have a "humanity" to be respected? Obviously what changed was not the physical or psychical features of those who were chastised. The change affected a conception of, and a sensibility towards, man as such, man stripped of all social, cultural, economic, and other, especially divine, attributes. The term "human" is not opposed to "animal" but to "divine." This secularization of power was accompanied by a desacralization of the recipient of punishment and victim of power, who lost his divine dimension and became weak. The reaction against torture was a result of a new way of looking at the victim of torture, who until then had been considered to be vested with the resilience of a god or a semi-god. His body no longer "doubled up" to receive punishment, the expression of an absolute power. The violence that went with the sacred was henceforth mitigated.

Secularization implies not only dispensing with a religious foundation but progressively dispensing with all foundations. The notion of thought as foundation is limited to the idea of being as a structure: being is thought of not in its unfolding and its finitude but rather as a permanent, stable, eternal structure. Secularization means acknowledging finitude.[107] Penal discourse has not reflected this acknowledgement. On the contrary, it has always proceeded as if it owned both the past, in trying to re-establish the equilibrium disturbed by the crime, and the future, in forgetting the actual life span of a human being. This lack of awareness on the part of penal law is a consequence of practicing a rational and conceptual philosophy, precisely the philosophy that has led to an aporia in penal law: "that [which] is most rational in punishment, namely that it fits the crime, is at the same time most irrational, namely, that it erases it."[108] Nothing is more rational, or tends more to rationality, than the notion of punishment - says Ricoeur - but the rationality it seeks is not to be found, for it establishes a link between two manifestly heterogeneous moments: the evil that has been suffered and inflicted (by punishment) and the wrong that has been committed (through crime).[109]

Nevertheless, despite all attempts to efface or disguise it behind other meanings, this aporia has not been completely abandoned. And in the face of this aporia there persists a need to look for foundations in a fruitless philosophical pilgrimage. For this reason we should try out a form of reflection seeking to put an end to the vicious circle of rationality-irrationality in penal law.

Hermeneutic thought is a reflection upon and from experience. It is a thought directed towards knowledge that already exists. It is a recollecting thought, which learns what already it knows. It offers us an alternative way to think of penal law: from within penal law but without attempting to legitimize it by means of new foundations. Rational and conceptual philosophy functions on the basis of judgments systematically linked one to another in a logical universe, whereas hermeneutic thought, while not renouncing its rational character, refers constantly to the experience it wishes to clarify. Through experience we become aware that things were not the way we thought. A person of experience is someone knowing the limits of his expectations and the uncertainty of his projects. "The experience is experience of human finitude. The truly experienced person is one who has taken this to heart, who knows that he is master neither of time nor the future."[110]

Hermeneutic thought distances itself not only from Hegelian metaphysical thought but also from positivist scientificism and structuralism. A distinctive feature of the latter is that it imposes rigid patterns of classification and description aimed, above all, at the formulation of governing principles, and to the detriment of any considerations of content. Taken to its most extreme consequences, the structuralist method reduces content to the level of the non-essential, for it places the subject in a position of abstract neutrality, establishing a clear boundary between the observer and the observed.

Hermeneutics is a form of reflection motivated mainly by ethics. It comes as a reaction to a world which began to resemble a world of total organization, a world representing "the triumph of the objectifying and calculating attitude as an expression of the metaphysical tendency to identify Being with what is present and controllable."[111] By this identification human existence is reduced to pure presence, calculability and manipulability.

Philosophical hermeneutics does not imply the interpretation of philosophical texts; rather, it presents interpretation as the fundamental issue of philosophy. Legal hermeneutics, stemming from philosophical hermeneutics, does not limit itself to the understanding of legal texts and materials, to the relationship between law and sentence. It considers the legal system to be a part of the world. Therefore, the interpreter of the law cannot limit himself to the written document, as if only this text were the object of his endeavors. Social institutions, principles, and non-written rules also comprise part of the text.[112]

Hermeneutics is not at ease with a way of thinking that fails to take into account the actual historical position of the observer. In the horizon of hermeneutic reflection, both observer and observed enter into play. Players are at the same time "played," and thinkers are "thought." No previous credentials are demanded of the players in order for them to play. And in the game, we take parts as we are and as we stand, with all our conditionings and prejudices.

"Prejudice" does not necessarily mean "false judgment." Prejudice simply refers to a judgment that has been pronounced before examining all the relevant elements. The fundamental prejudice of the Enlightenment, the prejudice against prejudices generally, is a reflection of the ideal of the "absolute self-construction of reason," which is itself, in turn, a prejudice.[113]However, human existence – says Gadamer – even the freest, is limited and conditioned in multiple ways. The ideal of absolute reason is not a possibility for historical humanity. Reason exists for us only as an actual and historical reason, which means that it is not its own master but remains contingent upon the given circumstances in which it operates.

Hence the inference that in order to account for man's historical and finite being, there is a need for a fundamental rehabilitation of prejudices and an acknowledgement that there are legitimate prejudices. Only by acknowledging the constitutive character of prejudices in each understanding will this understanding become a possibility. Only those prejudices of which we are unaware can cloud our understanding.[114] Legal interpretation always sets out from a set of assumptions, a background of implicit knowledge "whose incidence, in the past, has not been sufficiently reflected upon by legal thought, and to which legal hermeneutics is constantly drawing attention."[115]

Our coexistence with criminal law implies the preservation of a series of prejudices that form part of our historical and social reality, that have been received by us and that will probably, although not necessarily, be passed on by us. In other words, they have a temporal, finite, historical character. Philosophical hermeneutics invites us to become aware of these prejudices and to consider them from within their own historical perspective; it asks us neither to assign them to the category of foundations nor to seek other foundations to support them. It suggests that we should end our search for strong and structural legitimizing assumptions and instead undertake an interpretation of our present assumptions.

Interpretation develops in circular motion. One hermeneutic rule, for instance, states that the whole must be understood beginning from the parts, and the parts beginning from the whole. The anticipation of meaning that encompasses the whole becomes an explicit understanding insofar as the parts, which are determined by the whole, determine the whole as well. The movement of the understanding works constantly from the whole to the parts and from the parts to the whole. The unity of meaning extends or expands in concentric circles. For Heidegger, however, what characterizes the hermeneutic circle is that the understanding of the text is consistently determined by the anticipatory movement of fore-understanding. "A person who is trying to understand a text is always projecting. He projects a meaning for the text as a whole as soon as some initial meaning emerges in the text. Again, the initial meaning emerges only because he is reading the text with particular expectations in regard to certain meaning. Working out this fore-projection, which is constantly revised in terms of what emerges as he penetrates into the meaning, is understanding what is there." [116]

It is important to point out that the anticipation of meaning that guides our understanding is not merely a subjective act but an act determined by what we hold in common with tradition. This communality, however, is not an assumption established once and for all; rather, it unfolds in a continuous process. We ourselves establish it as we actively contribute to the maintenance and evolution of tradition; in such a way we carry it forward. "Thus, the circle of understanding is not a 'methodological' circle, but describes an element of the ontological structure of understanding."[117] Understanding is a constituent feature of human existence.

The concept of precomprehension is central to legal hermeneutics; "it is the engine that sets in motion the process of understanding, with a hypothesis of a possible meaning which will then allow itself to be constantly checked by subsequent hypotheses that adapt, improve or replace the initial one."[118] Out of the three hermeneutic circles that Alexy identifies, the first shapes the relationship between precomprehension and the text. The precomprehension is a hypothesis held by the interpreter that expresses his assumptions or expectations in relation to the correct solution of the legal problem. Its content is determined by the interpreter's general conception of society and by his own experiences. The image of the circle represents the interaction between the text of the provision and the interpreting hypothesis. To this circle corresponds the "reflexivity postulate."

The second circle encompasses the relationship between the parts and the whole. On the one hand, in order to understand a provision, it is necessary to understand the system of rules to which it belongs. On the other hand, it is not possible to understand the system without understanding the rules that make it up. The "coherence postulate" corresponds to this circle. It indicates that the notion of a legal system implies that "the judge's sentence must not arise from an unpredictable arbitrariness, but from the fair evaluation of the whole."[119] This implies that the issue is not one merely of formal coherence among the rules that make up a legal system but one of a coherence of content. This amounts to the "unity and interdependence of meaning of the legal discourse."[120]

According to Dworkin's conception of law as integrity, the sphere in relation to which the rule must remain coherent is larger still: the lawyer must test his interpretation of any part of a broad "network of political structures and community decisions by asking whether it could form part of a coherent theory justifying the network as a whole."[121] Zaccaria, on the other hand, refers to "a community of legal interpretation." The criterion that would determine the acceptability of the chosen interpretation would be premised upon reference to the interpretative community that linked together the members of a particular legal tradition.[122]

The third circle represents the relationship between rules and facts. The "completion postulate" corresponds to this circle. Legal hermeneutics says Zaccaria, is defined on the basis of the acknowledgement that an abstract rule reveals a structure that is necessarily incomplete and that can be completed only through the hermeneutic process of "concretization" of the legal rule in the context of the resolution of a particular case. This link between interpretation and application allows us to read the legal text in the light of the concrete situation to which it must be applied. The concrete situation ceases, then, to be a passive recipient of the application of the rule but instead determines the very meaning of the rule to be applied to it. This does not mean, as the author makes clear, granting a rule-making power to fact, or making the legal rule contingent upon a concrete case, but simply admitting that the legal rule, which cannot be chosen by the interpreter without some previous guidance on the facts to be judged, will not withstand separation, lest it suffer a decisive loss of legal power, from that section of social reality to which it refers.[123] The relationship established by legal hermeneutics between *Sollen* and *Sein* is both its fundamental contribution and a key proposition. "Only when *Sein* and *Sollen*, a concrete life relationship and one or several rules, come into reciprocal correspondence, only then can the concretization of the law take place. "[124]

All this shows the importance that philosophical hermeneutics attributes to application. Gadamer recalls that the earliest hermeneutic tradition distinguished between *subtilitas intelligendi,* the understanding; *subtilitas explicandi,* the explanation; and *subtilitas applicandi,* the application. They were considered the three constituent moments of interpretation, and the fact that they were called *subtilitas* meant that they were regarded not so much as methods as talents requiring a particular finesse of mind. Later on, Romanticism would acknowledge this intimate unity between *intelligere* and *explicare.* The explanation is not considered to follow the understanding; the understanding is always an explanation, this being the explicit form of the understanding. Gadamer observes that this intimate fusion of understanding and explanation had as a consequence the exclusion from hermeneutics of the third moment of interpretation: the application. The application of the Scriptures in Christian teaching and preaching was considered to be completely distinct from the historical and theological understanding of the Scriptures themselves. Instead, Gadamer submits that in understanding, some kind of application of the interpreted text always occurs; he believes that the application, along with the understanding and the explanation, is a constituent aspect of the interpretative act conceived as a unity. "In both legal and theological hermeneutics there is an essential tension between the fixed text – the law or the gospel – on the one hand, and, on the other, the sense arrived at by applying it at the concrete moment of interpretation, either in judgment or in preaching."[125] In the case of legal interpretation, "discovering the meaning of a legal text and discovering how to apply it in a particular legal instance are not two separate actions, but one unitary process."[126]

In this regard, Zaccaria points out that for a given example of human behaviour to be related to a legal "*fattispecie,*" two steps involving hermeneutic activities are indispensable. First, the interpreter, on the basis of the notion of law that constitutes the starting point in his approach to the case, transforms the factual circumstances into circumstances relevant to the law. Second, he relates the specific case, legally constructed and re-elaborated, to the abstract prescriptive model of the rule. The procedure has a circular character: a prescriptive model is the starting point that guides the interpreter in the selection, within the specific case, of the legally relevant circumstances; and a prescriptive model (not necessarily identical to the point of departure) is the end point. "The rule, while attributing legal connotations to the facts it embraces, is at the same time enriched by the connotations of historical novelty provided by those facts."[127]

In a similar sense Gadamer states that "the jurist is always concerned with the law itself, but he determines its normative content in regard to the given case to which it is to be applied."[128]

He gives the example of understanding an order: "An order exists only where there is someone to obey it. Here, then, understanding belongs to a relationship between persons, one of whom is to give the order. To understand the order means to apply it to the specific situation to which it pertains.... it is given its real meaning when it is carried out and concretized in accordance with its meaning."[129]

From all the preceding premises we can infer the fundamental role attributed by hermeneutics to the judge, given the acknowledgement that an abstract rule reveals a structure that is necessarily incomplete and one that becomes complete only in the decision process pertaining to a specific case. Nevertheless, as Gadamer puts it: "The creative supplementing of the law that is involved is a task reserved to the judge, but he is subject to the law in the same way as is every other member of the community. It is part of the idea of a rule of law that the judge's judgment does not proceed from an arbitrary and un-predictable decision, but from the just weighing up of the whole."[130] Osuna Fernández Largo also draws attention to the task of the judiciary and notes that hermeneutics "has made it clear that there is a need for a concrete application as an unavoidable aspect of the understanding of a rule that is both general and distant in time." And he adds: "Without reference to what is legally concrete and applied, it is not possible to understand the law. That is why the model of legal understanding is the judgment by the court, where the understanding of the rule and its relevance in a specific application of it are one."[131]

The judgment expresses a tension between the universality of the rule and the singularity of the specific case; a tension between the theoretical proposition and the praxis. It is necessary to close the gap between the universality of the law and the specific situation of the particular case. The essential characteristic of any legal system is to be flexible enough to provide leeway for its application to each individual case. This leeway must not end with the judgment that interprets and applies the law, or rather that interprets the law in its application. The sentence must also be applied and, therefore, interpreted. Gadamer states that the concrete outcome of a trial in a specific case does consists not only in the formulation of a theoretical proposition but also in "doing things with words." Thus it can be said, he adds, "that each application of the law goes beyond the mere understanding of its legal sense and fashions a new reality."[132]

This incidence of interpretation in the creation of reality is undoubtedly a source of responsibility for the interpreter of the law. When we talk about the importance attributed to application by hermeneutic philosophers, we are referring not only to the operation that covers the distance between the universal and the particular but to the distance between the formulation of a prescriptive statement, such as a judgment, and its practical application.

The application that we are concerned with here consists not in translating a general into a particular statement but in translating, if we can describe it as such, a linguistic proposition into concrete reality. This is what eventually will determine the prescriptive content of the law. If we consider a judgment to be the equivalent of an order, Gadamer's words will be applicable to it: "the true meaning of the order is determined in the concrete dimension of its proper execution." The true meaning of a sentence establishing a punishment is determined within the concrete dimension of the execution of the punishment. Each term in the sentence must be interpreted in relation to its practical application. And this application, in turn, will determine the meaning of each term.

The conditions of the execution of a punishment or, in other words, the conditions of the application of the sentence, will define the content of the former and the meaning of the latter. The interpretative work does not end in the formulation of the judgment. It is necessary to continue it beyond the sentence, until it has been translated into those actions, facts, and practical conditions that will fulfill it.

In many national legal systems, between the sentence and its execution there are frequently to be found additional rules that operate as bridges between the one and the other. They constitute the law of penal execution. Referring to the discipline that deals with this branch of law, Zaffaroni says that "it is just as necessary as the knowledge of penal law itself, because a punitive power that operates without prescriptive limits on the treatment that a person may be given from the moment the court pronounces its sentence until it lapses upon the termination of a prison term would imply [leaving] to discretionary power the most real aspect of punishment." He adds that this branch of law must be guided by the same interpretative principles that bind criminal law.[133]However, in many penal systems, even if these rules of execution do exist, the conditions in which punishment involving imprisonment are applied are so extreme that they entail the undergoing of many other punishments in addition to a deprivation of freedom.[134]

Let us return for a moment to the period when torture and corporal punishment were more commonplace. When the sentence that imposed them was executed, translating the rule into each specific case did not give rise to much difficulty. Regarding the first hermeneutic circle, precomprehension, or the expectations regarding the interpretation of the rule, these were fundamentally fulfilled, given that in those days cruelty in the application of a punishment did not contradict what was expected from the wielding of sovereign power. Regarding the second circle, the relationship between the parts and the whole, apparently there was nothing in the system of rules that would openly impede such a punishment. Lastly, regarding the third circle, the relationship between rule and action, it must be recalled that the cruelty of a punishment was meticulously stipulated in the rules of its execution, so that the application left more room for mitigating than for intensifying it.

We now face a completely different situation. In order to be consistent with the importance that we have assigned to application, we must reverse the order of the circles. We set out from the third circle, that involving the relationship between rule and action. This concerns the "completion postulate," since the meaning of a rule is "completed" by an action. In order to reply to a question about the meaning of the expression "deprivation of freedom," one must observe how such a punishment is translated into practice and under what conditions its execution is carried out. These conditions will indicate the meaning of "deprivation of freedom." When such conditions are so extremely precarious as to favour the transmission of illnesses, as well as all kinds of physical and psychic disturbances, including death, then by "deprivation of freedom" one should understand subjecting a convict to such extremely precarious conditions and, accordingly, to all the sufferings that they entail. I believe that there would be no objection to including the right not to be subjected to all these conditions under the label of "human rights," or to stating that a sentence that imposes this kind of submission is a rule that prescribes the violation of human rights.

Once the content of the sentence is defined, we can move on to the second hermeneutic circle, that of the relationship between the parts and the whole. Here one must examine each legal system to establish whether there are rules prohibiting the violation of human rights. If the answer is yes and if in no case such a violation is authorized, then a sentence that imposed a deprivation of freedom under conditions violating human rights would come into conflict with all the rules of the system that provided for the prohibition. Such a sentence, despite its formal validity, would therefore be inconsistent with the rules of the legal system under the framework in which it was issued. From a hermeneutic perspective, it would fail to observe the "coherence postulate" pertaining to this circle.

Next in our count backwards we arrive at the first circle. In the vast majority of countries belonging to the international community, all hypotheses that constitute our precomprehension of the rules are determined by a culture where human rights are "not expected" to be violated under the cover of the legal system or by virtue of its rules. We can refer to this expectation as the "human rights culture."[135] In it, the preliminary project that is elaborated in the precomprehension of the sentence does not anticipate the meaning that the sentence will finally adopt. In fact, it anticipates another meaning, which is more in agreement with the principles of a human rights culture but which does not correspond to the meaning the sentence has in its practical dimension. Insofar as this practical dimension is kept out of sight behind prison walls and insofar as the sufferings inflicted by the sentence, as opposed to torture, tend to remain alien to our everyday awareness, that other "precomprehended" meaning could paradoxically help us to forget the contradiction that exists at the heart of the "human rights culture," not only between our representations and the rules of the legal system but also between the rules themselves.

Our circles are disappointing.

Denouncing the higher likelihood of dying in prison, Neuman says: "A judge that deprives someone of his freedom is, even if he normally does not know it or think about it, somehow sentencing him to death."[136] Is it acceptable for a judge unknowingly or unthinkingly to sentence someone to death? What can be made of a legal system whose rules are flexible to the point of allowing such a possibility? On several occasions I have pointed out an analogy between prisons and concentration camps. The Nazis did not find it unbearable to live with Auschwitz. They had a philosophy to justify it, as Lévinas recalls in his masterly "Philosophy of Hitlerism."[137] Not only was there a set of beliefs that allowed them to live with such horror; there was also a set of laws that legitimized such a coexistence.

We may then ask what philosophy is it that allows us to live with horror? What leads us passively to pursue this coexistence, when we no longer have laws to justify it? When our laws expressly prohibit it, moreover?[138] Can we say also that we defend our behavior in a philosophy grounded, for instance, in a "myth of punishment," in a "sense of justice"? Or is it just for practical reasons, such as security, the desire to impose order and to free everyday life from uncertainty, that we passively accept such a violation of human rights?

Modern man continues to demand something of philosophy, says Vattimo, even though he may no longer expect structuring and objectifying thoughts. He demands its continuity in the face of two different kinds of deviation or discontinuance: first, between the present and the past; second, between the various knowledge's of the world, which in their growing specialization refuse to produce a synthesis.[139] In the face of the first deviation, philosophy should remind us that coexistence with punishment has a long history: we now coexist with prisons, just as our ancestors coexisted with torture, and in many countries we continue to coexist with capital punishment (a strange continuity between the past and the present: the most extreme form of punishment has remained a common element over time).

The awareness of this continuity, through a remembering thought, will weaken the foundations that still support punishment. It will show us its contingent, historical dimension. It will enable us to refuse to accept as inevitable structures the solutions currently imposed on us by the penal system. It will lead us to question whether we remain willing to continue to inherit the mythology of punishment, the notion of evil and expiation, as if they were eternal and immutable structures, rather than beliefs that we have received from our religious and cultural tradition. Recognizing what has been passed down to us simply as something transmitted, and nothing more, responds, in turn, to a process of secularization of thought, "a consummation of the strong, reassuring albeit violent features of being, with all the ethical and political implications that this involves."[140]This secularization of thought may also have opened the way to the notion of human rights, given that both secularization and human rights connote the vulnerability and fragility of being.

Regarding the second deviation, philosophy can perhaps help us to find some unity between the multiple specializations of knowledge, pointing to the need for each and every one of them to be accompanied by another, essential kind of knowledge: "One has to grasp the reason for the fact that alongside theory, alongside the all-consuming passion to know (which has its anthropological basis in the primitive fact of curiosity), there is another genuinely all-encompassing use of reason that consists not in learnable skill or blind conformism but in one's rational responsibility to oneself."[141] This answerable rationality is the guiding principle of hermeneutics. What exactly is this rationality? It is the capacity to overcome the dogmatic temptation that goes with all supposed knowledge. It is the clear and constant awareness of human finitude, of our own – and the other's – finitude. It is the acceptance of the fact that a reliance on the multiple specializations of knowledge as an answer to social problems can lead us to humanly abhorrent solutions, unless it is accompanied by this "answerable rationality," which is no more than an ability to respond, that human beings expect, or at least should be able to expect, from other human beings. Gadamer considers this notion of answerable rationality to be the fundamental hermeneutic virtue.

M. Ferraris begins his *History of Hermeneutics* by saying: "Hermes, the messenger of the gods, exercised a practical activity: the delivery of announcements, warnings, prophecies. In its mythical origins and in its following history, hermeneutics, as a transformative and communicative practice, is opposed to theory as contemplation of eternal essences unalterable by their observer."[142] Hermeneutics has an active role. A role that entails a responsibility: "Thinking that no longer understands itself as the recognition and acceptance of an objective, authoritarian foundation will develop a new sense of responsibility as ready and able, literally, to respond to others whom, insofar as it is not founded on the eternal structure of Being, it knows to be its 'provenance.'"[143]

For the moment penal thought has not ceased to acknowledge and to accept objective foundations, or to search for new foundations, to justify punishment. Hermeneutics will perhaps induce it to put an end to this search and to this acceptance, and to reason in a responsible way about the issues raised by the "penal problem"; above all, it will perhaps induce it to provide an urgent answer to the gap opened up between rules and reality that makes it possible for the State to become a criminal and for the criminal to become a victim.

Chapter Five

The Third Party: an Interpretation

"Zeus ... sent Hermes to bring justice and a sense of shame to humans, so that there would be order within cities and bonds of friendship to unite them. Hermes asked Zeus how he should distribute shame and justice to humans. 'Should I distribute them as the other arts were? This is how the others were distributed: one person practicing the art of medicine suffices for many ordinary people; and so forth with the other practitioners. Should I establish justice and shame among humans in this way, or distribute it to all?' 'To all', said Zeus, 'and let all have a share. For cities would never come to be if only a few possessed these, as is the case with the other arts'."[144]

Law is born of conflict: in the existence of current conflict and in the possibility of future conflict. Its structure is antithetical. Conflict presupposes the presence of two conflicting parties. Resolving the conflict means putting an end to the conflict between these two parties.

A confrontation denotes a relationship, but this relationship involves a particular kind of reciprocity, a reciprocity of exclusion. A confrontation implies a relationship that aims at the total exclusion of the other.[145] This reciprocity of exclusion is, therefore, a temporary condition that is bound to end with the final exclusion of one or other of the conflicting parties. At this level, the relationship takes place in the realm of the imaginary, which consists in the identification of what exists with the fixedness of an image, an image that can equally belong to oneself or to someone else, or to the world. In the imaginary, the being is situated in a twofold relationship: the I and the self, the I and the other, the I and the world. This is always a direct relationship, one that is not mediated.[146]

A confrontation implies a spatial dimension, a face-to-face. This face-to-face connotes, in turn, a certain threat; the threat of an encounter between the conflicting parties. It is necessary to avoid the threat of proximity between the opponents. There is an urgent need for distance, and the only person who can establish this distance is someone other than the antagonists: a third party

> who creates the possibility of drawing a distinction between the self, the other, and the world. The presence of the third party puts all existence and coexistence at the level of the symbolic. The third party makes it possible to overcome the imaginary and transcend into the symbolic, since it cannot be identified with the image of either party in the relationship. In keeping and preserving the difference between both sides, he maintains and preserves each one of the parties and, therefore, the relationship itself, investing it with duration. In other words, he embodies the primary goal of law: to free the relationship from the anxiety of the unforeseen. He signals the correspondence between "the symbolic" and the law.[147]

The third party plays a role throughout the entire scope of the legal phenomenon. The third party's function is present from the inception of the development of the contents of the law, namely, the legislative activity, until the final concrete fulfillment of the law, namely, the judicial activity. "Thus, the legal phenomenon manifests itself as a relationship mediated by a third party."[148] Here we shall discuss the role of the third party in judicial activity.

The presence of the third party is the keynote in the administration of justice. Who is the third party whom we entrust with the administration of justice? What do we ask of him? How does the third party proceed in order to give us what we demand while at the same time remaining a third party? What is the third party's place? Where does he position himself? Above all, it is necessary to specify where he must not be positioned. He must not be located in any of the places occupied by the conflicting parties but must rather be at a point that is equidistant from both of them. In order to find this equal distance, he must position himself at the centre. "When disputes arise, therefore, men appeal to the judge: and an appeal to the judge is an appeal to that which is just; for the judge is intended to be, as it were, a living embodiment of that which is just; and men require of a judge that he shall be moderate [or observe the mean], and sometimes even call judges 'mediators,' signifying that if they get the mean they get that which is just. That which is just, then, must be a sort of mean, if the judge be a 'mediator.' "[149]

Nevertheless the position of the third party-judge, in the middle, which allows him to keep separate the conflicting parties, also allows him to maintain his own "distance" from them. It is essential for him not to get closer to one party than to the other. And in distancing himself from both, he must also be distant from anything that in itself might incline him to assume a "partial" position, shortening the distance separating him from either party.

The concept of impartiality is purely introspective. According to Kojève, when we say that someone is impartial with regard to A and B, we mean that he does not favour one over the other, but also that he does not feel love or hatred for either. A proof of the third party's impartiality is that his intervention would not vary if A and B were interchanged. Impartiality, however, involves not only the third party's attitude regarding the conflicting parties but also his attitude towards the conflict itself. In this respect, the just distance means the place where the third party must be positioned in order to have a correct view of the conflict. It is said that he must not be interested: he must not have any personal interest in the outcome of the conflict. This implies that the resolution of the conflict would not bring to him either gain or loss. As far as he is concerned, he would remain in the same situation as before. His action would not affect him in any way. Kojève notes also, however, that this assertion has no real value. The intervention of the third party is, by definition, an action, and, as such, it modifies the world. This modification always has an impact upon those living in the modified world. This modified world is also the world where the third party lives. In addition, the third party finds himself within a specific group at a specific time in his historical existence. Observed from outside the group, the third party will appear concerned with the group and its preservation. If his intervention affects the group in a negative way, he too will be affected. Kojève concludes by stating that an act is never disinterested. The third party cannot be disinterested, for he will always suffer, directly or indirectly, the consequences of his action.[150]

No one would accept, however, a resolution that came from a third party who was interested in a particular outcome, either in favour of or against either party. Thus, an alternative way is sought to establish whether the third party's intervention is disinterested or not: his intervention is deemed to be disinterested if it remains unchanged even when the third party is replaced by another. If both the former and the substitute third parties intervene as if they are not affected by their involvement, that is, as if are not two different persons, as if there is just one intervening third party, then it could be said that the intervention of either is disinterested.

The substitutability of the third party leads us to the concept of "anybody."[151] Actually, "anybody" cannot really be anybody: no society would ever consent to a madman or child acting as third party. Nevertheless, we do mean something by the term. Husserl points out that "anybody" is not an abstract concept or a conceptual common denominator to which we refer the multiplicity of individual human beings. Instead, it is a concrete concept; it is "every man" considered with respect to what he has in common with all other men. "The condition of being 'anybody' eliminates the variations of human nature, but not human nature itself.... At some level of our being, every one of us is 'anybody'"[152]

The question that should be asked, then, is the following: how has this man behaved in this particular situation? If the answer is that in that particular situation he behaved as any one of us would, then the concept of "objectivity" can enter into play in the description of such behavior. This concept means that what gives sense to behavior is the thing itself, namely, "the object of the conflict," and not the individual preferences or prejudices.[153]

In order to find a perspective from which to observe the thing as it really is, it is essential for the third party to distance himself from his inner self, which is locked in his own preferences, dislikes, and prejudices. Prejudices can block access to the thing that is to be considered. But what are prejudices? For the law, a prejudice is a decision that precedes final judgment. For the party in relation to which the prior decision is unfavorable, prejudice involves narrowing down his chances of winning. In this regard, prejudice equals limitation, disadvantage, and harm.

Another meaning attributed to "prejudice" is that of an unfounded judgment. Only through foundation and verification by means of method will a judgment acquire validity. Gadamer recalls, however, that the Latin term *praejudicium* means simply "adverse effect," "disadvantage," "harm." "But this negative sense is only derivative. The negative consequence depends precisely on the positive validity, the value of the provisional decision as prejudgment, like that of any precedent."[154] Prejudice does not necessarily mean a false judgment. Prejudice means only a judgment pronounced before examining all the relevant elements. Human existence, says Gadamer, even at its freest, is limited and conditioned in multiple ways. "What appears to be a limiting prejudice from the viewpoint of the absolute self-construction of reason in fact belongs to historical reality itself. If we want to do justice to man's finite, historical mode of being, it is necessary to fundamentally rehabilitate the concept of prejudice and acknowledge the fact that there are legitimate prejudices."[155]

Prejudices draw a horizon. They form the fence that embraces and encompasses all that can be seen, all that is visible from a specific viewpoint. The concept of horizon is flexible: one may refer to a limiting of the horizon, to an expansion of the horizon, or to an opening up of new horizons. The parties in conflict endure a limiting of their horizon. They cannot go beyond the situation to which they are linked by conflict. In their particular situation, they can see only as far as the boundaries which limit their horizon. Thus, they cannot see clearly, fairly. In order to resolve the conflict, a third party must acquire the just horizon. In order to achieve this, however, he must not abandon his own horizon. From his own horizon, he must try to understand those past events that were at the origin of the conflict. He must bring those past events back into the minds of the parties. He must go through them over again, live them anew, experience them today. He must transpose himself into the historical horizon in which the incidents took place. But what does "transpose himself" mean? It implies not a disregarding of oneself but rather a placing of oneself in an alien situation.[156] We will become aware of the other, of the unrelenting individuality of the other, of his "otherness," only if we put ourselves in his situation. Nevertheless, the third party must never lose consciousness of his own situation, of his own historical horizon, of his own prejudices.

However, we all experience limitations to our horizons. The time itself in which we live limits our horizon, the horizon of our present. The horizon of the present is continually to be formed or in the process of being formed. The horizon of the present in which the third party operates is always actual: it is continually in the making. The third party, a bridge between the parties, acts in the present, a bridge across time. Between the facts of the past and the facts of the future, it is necessary to create an encounter in the present. The present is where a relationship is established between the conflict or crime, which belongs to the past, and the resolution of the conflict, or the penal consequence of the crime, which belongs to the future. The third party must redirect events from the past into the present and then observe their projection into the future. He faces temporality in its triple synthetic presence: "*praesens de praeteritis, praesens de praesentibus, praesens de futuris.*"[157] The third party must produce this temporal unity before his own eyes, before the eyes of the parties, and before the eyes of society. The present is also "third" in relation to the other temporal dimensions.[158]

Thus, the distance separating the parties has not only a spatial but also a temporal dimension. In the process, a "reaction" to an action is stopped, and the relationship between the conflicting parties is established at another level, where the relationship develops at a different pace. The third party breaks up the pairing of action and reaction. He aims to substitute his own intervention for the parties' immediate reactions, thereby slowing the reaction time. We could say, therefore, that his involvement is an intervention not only in space but also in time: "The immediate deadly impulse is followed by the deferred time of the process; each one will be invited to verbalize their claims. "[159]

The conflict is "verbalized," expressed through a discourse translating the claims of both parties. The rules that govern the discourse define the functions of each participant in the trial and establish the limits of their respective roles. The third party judge interprets the parties' discourses (the word "interpret" containing "inter," "in-between," and "in the middle of," a reflection of the position he occupies). His position, too, is between "the positions of the discourses." His intervention will likewise be expressed in words. Each party pronounces his own discourse, although that of the third party is not completely his own. Since he acts on behalf of the legal community; his discourse must be grounded in the laws of that community. This implies that he cannot, in theory, solve the conflict according to his own free will.

His action can be described using the concept of "*dispositio in ordinem*" (an expression borrowed from architecture describing the action of the architect as he builds). This way of ordering facts means giving each fact its legal name: "to reconcile words and things."[160] In order to do this, he must direct his gaze "on the things themselves." According to Gadamer, "A person who is trying to understand a text is always projecting. He projects a meaning for the text as a whole as soon as some initial meaning emerges in the text."[161] The third party, from his specific position, is able to "project" a possible solution to the conflict that the parties, constrained as they are by their own respective positions, are incapable of seeing. The term "projecting" has here a temporal connotation, a connotation of the future.

The application of the law also reveals a confluence in time between the past to which the law belongs and the present in which it is applied. "The legal rule enters historical time. The flow of time does not stop. And the rule, we can say, moves along with it."[162] Time is not an abyss that must be crossed over because it separates and creates distance but the foundation of all that comes to pass. Temporal distance, therefore, is not something that must be overcome. It is not an abyss extending before us, but rather something filled with the continuity of transmission. "Here it is not too much to speak of the genuine productivity of the course of events."[163] According to Gadamer, the application of the law is not an accidental and additional application of a general principle to a concrete case that has already been understood in a specific way. The application represents the proper understanding of the universal itself, which for us is the text of the law to be applied. Each law, because of its universal character, implies an inevitable disparity in relation to concrete actions. The law is always deficient, not in itself, but because it aims at regulating the reality of the human world, which in itself is variable, unpredictable, and imperfect. A pure and straightforward application of the law is impossible because circumstances are infinite and whoever applies the law must perceive them in their infinite variety.

Gadamer compares the application of the law to the work of a craftsman. He has the rules, and there is a project he must carry out. As he begins his work, specific circumstances may force him to depart from the project as initially conceived. In such a case he will have applied his knowledge, but even so the work will end up being imperfect. Whoever "applies justice" or administers justice, says Gadamer, faces a quite different situation. He too will have to refrain from applying the full rigor of the law. However, when this happens, it will not be because he cannot do better, but because if he acted in any other way he would not be right. "In restraining the law," says Gadamer, "he is not diminishing it but, on the contrary, finding the better law."[164]

In view of the need to correct the strict application of the law, a question arises: what rules must the third party-judge abide by when he applies the rules? The answer to this question is, "there are no rules for the reasonable use of rules.""In fact," says Gadamer, "the logical basis of judgment – subsuming a particular under a universal, recognizing something as an example of a rule – cannot be demonstrated. Thus judgment … cannot be taught in the abstract but only practiced from case to case, and is therefore more an ability like the senses."[165] Gadamer recalls that Aquinas considered common sense to be the common root of the other senses, in other words, the faculty that combined them. And common sense is decisively characterized by the ability to make judgments. Furthermore, he adds, the introduction of the term "ability to judge" in the eighteenth century aimed at properly conveying the Latin concept of *judicum*, understood as a basic spiritual gift. "It is something that cannot be learned, because no demonstration from concepts can guide the application of rules."[166]

The third party-judge is positioned at a crossing point between the universality of the rule and the singularity of the case. It is the point that Ricoeur describes as "the tragic dimension of action," where the conflict is no longer between people who are parties, or between rules that offer different answers, but between "the respect owed to the universal norms" and "the respect owed to singular persons."[167] It must also to be understood that justice is always addressed to singularities, to the singularity of the other, in spite or even because of its presumed universality.[168]

It is precisely in the resolution of this conflict between the universal and the particular that the creativity of the third party-judge is made manifest. He is entrusted with the task of perfecting the meaning of the rule, which remains structurally incomplete until applied to a concrete case.[169]

Still, in its application the judge not only acts upon the law by completing its meaning; he also modifies the concrete reality. The words of his decision have a direct impact upon reality. Along with Gadamer, we can say that on issuing his judgment, the judge not only formulates a theoretical proposition but also "does things with words."[170] With this activity comes responsibility for the third party-judge-interpreter. "The interpreter is invested with the responsibility and the function of transforming the "abstract reasonability" of the rule into the "concrete reasonability" of the decision."[171] This is the "rationality" or "responsibility" referred to by Gadamer. What is it? What do we mean by someone being reasonable? We mean "that he has overcome the temptation of dogmatism that goes with all supposed knowledge. So someone can strive for what he wants and try to bring it about through his actions, but he must always find his ground in the givens of our finite Dasein."[172]

And then there is the judgment of Solomon. Carbonnier refers to it as "the famous judgment, as if there had been no others, although the biblical narrator says that Solomon pronounced three thousand … But we do not know much about the remaining 2999."[173] Why was this judgment so extraordinary as to be engraved forever upon our memories? Solomon was only twenty-three years of age. His genius, according to Carbonnier, came from an intuitive wisdom rather than from experience or from knowledge of precedents. He reminds us that the apparently civil proceedings on filiations, on the determination of the identity of a living child, given that two mothers were fighting over it, concealed a latent criminal procedure. "Mothers not only litigated about possession (of the child), but also about their own innocence, maybe their own lives." (Because if there had also been a dead child and if the child had been stifled by his own mother, the absence of willfulness, the involuntary character of the homicide, would not have been a mitigating circumstance in that particular legal system.) Solomon pronounces his verdict: "cut the living child in half and give one half to each woman." Solomon was here doing nothing more than applying Hebraic law, which stipulated the splitting of the object in dispute.

The peculiarity of the judgment resides in its having been used as a means of proof. One can wonder, however, Is it really the judge's ingenuity that has made this verdict persist in our memories? Or is it the cleverness of testing the parties by pronouncing a sentence that stipulated the destruction of the disputed object itself? Or the horror provoked by the possibility that the sentence could actually have been applied? Or the reaction to the threat of cutting a human being in two? Many similar horrors have been recorded by the history of jurisprudence …

I believe, instead, that the judgment has remained in our memories because it is a sentence establishing the division of something indivisible. It demonstrates the pointlessness of the division for each of the parties in dispute, given that the desired "object" would cease to be, precisely as a consequence of having stopped "being." The sentence demonstrates the absurdity inherent in the application of distributive justice where there is in fact nothing that could be distributed.

Another peculiar feature of the judgment is that it resorts to death as a solution to the problem without referring to death as such. Nevertheless, with his sentence, Solomon brought the possibility of death into the consciousness of the parties. He relied on this awareness; he trusted it to solve the conflict. This is what Solomon's wisdom is all about. It is not about a presumed faculty to distinguish between good and evil but about an action founded on human finitude.

The third party-judge is also a human being. Although in many cases he will be able to resolve conflict and to give each one their just deserts, in other cases his involvement will be only a means to express outrage, repulsion, and pain. Solomon demonstrated that he could not solve the conflict by cutting the surviving child in half and then distributing one half to each mother; nor can a judge restore a situation that existed before a crime by then distributing suffering by means of the application of a punishment. An awareness of this impossibility and the acknowledgement of one's own powerlessness to undo what has already been done and to divide what is indivisible is what manifests the true wisdom of the third party-judge, the interpreter who understands and projects.

Chapter Six

Some Reflections on Penal Thought

The question concerning the law and the question concerning man are interdependent: neither can be formulated without the other. The law implies man and man the law. The question concerning the law and the question concerning man together form a fundamental part of philosophical enquiry.

The philosophical enquiry addressed to law is different from scientific systematization. The philosophy of law is never a systematization of legal knowledge directed towards the constitution of a scientific system. The philosophy of law originates in answer to the question of the meaning of law, a question that goes beyond a perspective which analyses it merely as technique. The key to the philosophy of law thus defined is the concept of possibility,[174] which points towards the boundary between the specific modality of man's being, insofar as he exists, and the world of the non-human, of other living beings and things. The law has its roots in possibility, in its subject wriggling out of the external determination of natural laws, in his exposure to the future. This exposure, which is inherent in the human being, is the source of that uncertainty which accompanies man to his death. The inability to elude such a possibility implies "not being able not to choose," as a need which is neither mathematical nor causal but which constitutes the inescapable nature of human being. Law emerges in the face of this inescapable necessity to choose and in the face of the resulting uncertainty for relationships of coexistence.[175]

The law expresses a need for certainty arising from the uncertainty inherent in human freedom. Nietzsche's cry in the *Genealogy of Morals* is worth recalling: "To ordain the future in advance in this way, man must first have learned to distinguish necessary events from chance ones, to think causally, to see and anticipate distant eventualities as if they belonged to the present, to decide with certainty what is the goal and what the means to it, and in general be able to calculate and compute. Man himself must first of all have become *calculable, regular, necessary*, even in his own image of himself, if he is to be able to stand security for *his own future*, which is what one who promises does!"[176]

This way of conceiving the world and oneself, inspired by the need for security and certainty, is typical of modernity. In modernity the representation of the world itself as a conceived image and of the constitution of man as subject, are crucial. Representation allows the whole entity to unfold before one's eyes and then to be fixed in its position. This is how scientific reasoning proceeds; it is also the method of the calculating man, who wishes to be sure, to acquire certainty. Only through calculation can the expected, enduring certainty of the representation, of that which is represented, be guaranteed. Representation is an enquiring and dominating form of objectification, since it objectifies what is represented in order to research, analyze, study, and dominate it. And in this representation, both the man who represents and the entity represented exist simultaneously.

It was precisely the man who could "represent" who became subject. And as subject, "is it necessary for him to confront, as a consequence, this explicit question: is it as an 'I' that is reduced to its random desires and abandoned to an arbitrary free-will or as the 'we' of society; is it as individual or as community; is it as a personal being within the community or as a mere member of the body corporate; is it as a state, nation, or people or as the indifferent humanity of modern man, that man wills and must be that subject which, *as* the essence of modernity, he *already* exists"[177] In other words, by setting himself up as the subject of representation, man could also conceive an image of himself, in order to represent himself as he wished and thus also to enter, himself, into the realm of what is calculable, securable, and available.

In order to enter into this realm, however, the subject had first to overcome the uncertainty that characterizes the world of experience. The world of experience is a world where doubt prevails and uncertainty and the unforeseen. The purpose of law is to secure relationships in the face of the possibility that they may be destroyed by the unexpected, to free them from the anxiety of a possible and unexpected destruction, and, in short, to invest them with duration. In this way the law is a tool with which to overcome anxiety: anxiety as a profound uneasiness about the future. It is a tool to save the relationship with the other from sinking into nothingness because of an unexpected mutation in the determination of one or other of its constituent parts.

In order to achieve this goal, legal thought moves the man of flesh and blood from a "realm of doubt" into a realm in which another, distinct temporality prevails.[178] And in this move it creates its own subject: it conceives the "subject of law." The temporality in which this subject exists emerges as "duration." In it, all three stages of time – present, past, and future – appear as a continuum. The law gives a unity of meaning to events that follow one after another in stages of time, when without such a meaning they would not constitute a unity.[179]

In contrast the human person, even before being conceived as a subject of law and in spite of an existence that unfolds through the three stages of time, does indeed constitute a unity. He is already a unity of meaning: he does not need the law to confer on him such a meaning. In him, the present, past, and future acquire a single continuity. As Pareyson remarks, the person, at each instant in his history, is, on the one hand, what he already is and, on the other, what he must yet become: "Sempre conclusa e aperta a un tempo" (always and at once both concluded and open). Thus, in the person totality and insufficiency are bound together. The person, insofar as *conclusa* in the present moment, is a totality, i.e., a point-by-point concentration of a succession of acts, decisions, deeds. However, insofar as none of his instants are final, he is insufficient and incomplete, a perennial opening to the future, a perpetual variation of instants. "A person is a totality in so far as he is the unity of his acts and an insufficiency in so far as he embodies always the possibility of fresh action." The person is himself, and yet must still be another, and this other that he must be will still be himself. According to Pareyson, these are a person's two extreme moments: the "must be," which is the start and the beginning, and the "already being," which is the completion and the end.[180] Doctrines justifying punishment are introduced in relation to these two moments. The first major classification of these doctrines is based upon a temporal distinction: *quia peccatum*, or doctrines that look to the past, and *ne peccetur*, or doctrines that look to the future.

It would be impossible to find a point of convergence between these doctrines. The fact that some of them look to the past and some to the future not only gives them a different temporal perspective but also sets them at two different levels whose points of intersection can never be found: the symbolic and the practical. Our actions may be projected into the future; we enjoy the possibility of exerting some influence upon a future reality. But our deeds can do nothing to change the past. They can only be projected into the past at a symbolic or imaginary level. "The free circulation of time is forbidden to man."[181] The will is powerless against what has been. The will trips over the stone of that which was. The '*it was*' is the stone that the will never be able to turn. "Eternally still stands the past." What has already been stands against any will. That is why there is in the will itself an aversion to what is averse to it, an aversion (*Widerwille*) against that which was. This aversion is, following Nietzsche, the essence of revenge. "This, indeed this alone, is what *revenge* is: the will's ill will against time and its 'it was.'"[182] Nevertheless, according to Heidegger, "The revulsion turns not against the mere passing, but against that passing away which allows what has passed to be only in the past, which lets it freeze in the finality of this *rigor mortis.*"[183]

Revenge, says Nietzsche, never calls itself by its own name, it calls itself "punishment,", thus disguising its hostile essence as law.[184] Beyond the highly debated issue of punishment as revenge, Nietzsche's words touch upon a very profound aspect of penal thought. They present punishment to us in its most primitive aspect, not just as a reaction to an unwanted and disapproved of act but as a reaction to an act that occurred even though it should not have occurred and that nevertheless cannot be cancelled because it has been impressed upon the past, "frozen in the finality of this *rigor mortis.*"

According to Husserl the core of all judicial activity consists in restoring a situation that would have existed had the rules not been violated. The principle that guides the judge's intervention is the idea of "status quo."[185] In a way, the purpose of law is to cancel out a past that does not conform to the rules. Thus, the law's gaze towards the past is both omnipotent and pretentious. Punishment is the expression of this will to dominate the past, which can be achieved only in a realm constructed by reason and imagination. For there is no direct path from the past into the future, nor vice versa. If one wished to take such a path, which in fact is beyond human reach, it would be necessary to do so with the imagination. The crime as an act of the past must be "made present."[186] Reason and imagination must carry out an exercise in abstraction to allow what has already occurred to again become present. But since it is impossible to turn the past into the present (except through memory), the past action is "converted" into a specific act characterized by the law in a specific way.

"If crime and its removal, or, more definitely, punishment, are regarded merely as evil, it might indeed be thought unreasonable to will a second evil merely because one already existed."[187] Thus, the injury is considered not only as an evil, a mere injury inflicted upon an individual subject: "The only thing that matters is that the crime must be done away with not as a sudden eruption of evil but as an injury to the law itself."Once the representation has been formed, the calculative thinking looks also for precision and clarity with respect to the relationship it establishes between the injury caused by the crime and that caused by the punishment.

As Ricoeur points out, "Nothing, indeed, is more rational, or at least nothing puts in more of a claim to rationality, than the notion of punishment. Crime merits chastisement, says the collective consciousness. ... The paradox is that this presumed rationality, which we shall call the logic of punishment, is an undiscoverable rationality."[188] The meaning of punishment as the conjunction of submission and forcing submission resides, says Ricoeur, in the presumed equivalence between, on the one hand, evil suffered and inflicted and, on the other hand, evil committed. This equivalence, he adds, constitutes the rationale of punishment. But what "is most rational in punishment, namely that it fits the crime, is at the same time most irrational, namely, that it erases it." [189] Ricoeur considers that Hegel has definitively demonstrated that the law of punishment is valid only in a limited sphere, which he calls "abstract right." The one condition for resolving "the enigma of punishment" is that the logic of punishment remains enclosed within the limits of the philosophy of right,[190] in other words, within the limits of representation created by reason and imagination.

The logic of punishment develops between two processes: a process of *detemporalization*, in which the "raw" act is abstracted from its own time, the past, and a process of *retemporalization*, by which the past act is "made present," although transformed into a legally defined act, with a view to "cancelling" the "raw" act that has taken place.

These two processes also apply to the author of the act. The human being, like his acts, is also "detemporalized" and "re-temporalized." In this process the main purpose is "to efface the crime," "to annihilate the unlawful act." To this end, a punishment is measured out in relation to the seriousness of the crime. And this measurement seeks to establish an equivalence between the crime and the punishment. But this equivalence can be found only in the temporal realm created by law. In it, the "duration" of a punishment does not coincide with the "duration" of the life of the being of flesh and blood. The legal subject does not reflect the human person in its most basic characteristic: its finitude.

Forgetting human finitude (his "not being forever") paves the way for the application of punishments exceeding a human life span. When this happens, the symbolic aspect of punishment acquires the dimension of the imaginary. Forgetting this "not being forever" conceals a perception of death which is also inspired by the calculations of legal thought and which sees it as just one more piece of data with respect to the abstract subject of law. From this perspective, death assumes the quality of an impersonal event. "One" dies, just as "one" enters into a contract, "one" fulfils an obligation, and so on. "One" gives the impression that whoever dies is an anonymous person. Actually, as Heidegger says, "one" corresponds to "no one." And "no one" not only does not have a name; he does not exist either. Death has become dissociated from concrete time and individuals. Thus dissociated from the individual, death is considered just another event. However, nothing is more unique and peculiar to the individual than his own death. His death is part of his "not being forever," which escapes all calculation and expectation and which is irreconcilable with certainty.

As we see, the law's imaginative gaze is directed not only towards the past. Indeed, some claim that the law's gaze is directed entirely towards the future, so that even when it looks back to the past, it does so with a view to performing its role of planning the future, a role that is crucial to ensuring the continuity of legal relationships, this being one of their essential elements. And without continuity there would be no relationships. In order to ensure its continuity, the law seeks to plan out the future. Instead of waiting passively for the future to happen, it actively engages with it, with resolution. "The journey of the law is the journey of a positive conquest of the future by means of the instruments of rationality."[191]

The "reasonable" goal of punishment is directed towards the future. This goal consists in putting an end to the unleashing of violence. Hegel: "As revenge is only the positive act of a particular will, it is a new injury. Through this contradiction it develops into an infinite process, the insult being inherited without end from generation to generation."[192] In order to avoid such a process towards infinity and an endless transmission of violence, a distance is interposed between victim and victimizer. "It is the just distance between partners who confront one another," says Ricoeur, "too closely in cases of conflict and too distantly in those of ignorance, hate, and scorn, that sums up rather well … the two aspects of the act of judging. On the one hand, to decide, to put an end to uncertainty, to separate the parties; on the other, to make each party recognize the share the other has in the same society."[193]

The objective of the trial is precisely to establish this "just distance." In such a context, it is worth recalling Kojève's interpretation of the third party: for society to exist, two human beings are as deficient as a single isolated being. The intervention of a third party is required. Since the law is an essentially social phenomenon, it t establishes not a direct relationship between subjects but rather one which is "mediated" by a third party: "The interaction between two human beings is not enough. The intervention of an impartial and disinterested third party is necessary as well."[194] The third party is present from the inception of the development of the legal rule, i.e., in legislative activity, until the final moment, when the law is made manifest, in judicial activity. According to this broad interpretation the term "third party" refers also to the law insofar as it is an expression of an intention that things should occur in a particular way.

Nevertheless, the figure of the third party is seen most clearly in the judge. And it is precisely the judge who will set in motion all the temporal processes to be unfolded from within penal thought. "The fact, the act, the will (and therefore the person) that are before him and that he must get to know, to examine, to discern and eventually to judge, are found in the past, as is the law on the basis of which he will judge. However, he must bring them from the past into the present, and see their extension into the future. "[195] It is the judge who must make manifest before his very own eyes, the eyes of the parties, and the eyes of society at large a temporal unity. And it is precisely because this synthetic truth remains alien to his personal conscience that he is capable of acting in agreement both with his raison d'être and with his position as third party.

In addition, the judge represents the State. Kojève's analysis of the role of the State in the penal context is of particular interest. On the one hand, the State deems itself injured by the crime; on the other, it acts as a third party. However, there is a degree of inconsistency between these two roles: if it is the victim, it cannot act as third party, and from the moment it acts as third party, it cannot claim the status of victim. In the face of this inconsistency, a distinction is established between the roles played here by the State and by society. The State acts as a third party, and society takes on the status of the victim, a distinction reflected in the different bodies involved in the trial: one has the authority to pursue the criminal in court, another is empowered to punish him.[196] In the framework of representations, we can see that not only is society assigned the role of victim in a given crime, but it is also regarded as a collection of people that includes the likely perpetrators of future crimes. In this sense, it becomes the addressee of the dissuasive message that the punishment is intended to convey.

In light of this situation, it would seem that society has internalized the individual both as current victim and as future criminal. And even though punishment will fall upon the individual, he performs a merely instrumental role in order that the message may reach those for whom it is intended. The individual, the man of flesh and blood, does not really exist in penal thought.

I said at the outset that the question concerning the law and the question concerning man were mutually supportive. This is the case only when the philosophical question concerning law is truly posed as a question that, in a critical manner, questions the law's approach to human beings. Romano, for instance, has pointed out that under the banner of the *pure theory of law*, the whole question of law boils down to asking which law is in force. Such a circumscribed question, not for what it asks but for what it does not ask, gives expression to a philosophy of law that purports to follow the model of scientific thought but that is blinded by its own alleged rigor and accuracy. Referring to theories that are limited to the formal structure of rules, Romano argues that they provide a "commonplace" reading of the law. "The original aim in constructing a pure doctrine of law, namely one freed of any ethical, sociological, political or psychological dimension, revealed itself to be flawed because it stopped itself from embracing the whole phenomenon of law, present in its full phenomenological dimension."[197]

Pareyson observes that as humanity emerged from the abyss of evil and suffering into which it had fallen during the Second World War, where it had touched what he regards as the most horrid point of wickedness, with utterly diabolical forms of perversion, with massacres and atrocious genocides, with unheard-of and heinous forms of suffering inflicted by men on men, precisely then did philosophies concerned with extremely abstract and subtle technical problems, philosophies that were insensitive to the issues of evil and suffering and that were in general barely interested in the problems of man and his destiny, such as logical positivism and analytical philosophy, precisely then did they attain such great success and such vast popularity.[198] This reaction to the response of philosophical thinking to concrete historical facts should also be voiced against the response of legal doctrine to those situations which are the concern of criminal law. Even acknowledging a legitimate search for intellectual purity, for freedom from all emotional conditioning, one cannot legitimize such a disregard for man's tragic plight in his relationship with evil, both as author and as recipient, as victim and as executioner. However, when, confronted by evil, philosophy has found no better solution, says Pareyson, than to suppress what is bothersome and to resolve the incomprehensible in clear rationality. A rationalist philosophy will never willingly accept that reason cannot dissipate all clouds, that it falls short before the opaque. Unable to cancel evil as negative reality, it incorporates it into a larger picture in which it is extremely mitigated, and minimized, and even disappears.

Something similar happens to philosophy of law in relation to criminal law. Instead of reflecting upon the drama in which it is caught up because of the very situations it is intended to respond to, because of how it has responded in the past, and because of the responses it has yet to provide, it tries increasingly to formalize its thinking with regard to penal rules. These rules maintain a very peculiar relationship to their recipient. As we have seen, on the one hand they detemporalized both him and his act, endowing him with an eternity he does not actually have, in order that the duration of the punishment may correlate with the seriousness of the crime. On the other hand, in their desire to plan ahead, they turn him into a mere vehicle of the message they wish to convey. What can be hoped for from a system of rules displaying such a lack of imagination?

In fact, this question begs another: what can be expected of a philosophy of law that does not reflect upon a system of rules set up in this way? A system of rules that does not reflect upon all these representations constructed by legal thought, distancing itself from the individual beings it addresses? A system of rules that simply accepts all these constructions as if they were evidence of an unchangeable reality and the basis for its further reflection?

However, the problem is not just to reflect upon the representational thinking that distances the law from its recipient. There is also an inescapable need to reflect upon the consequences that such thinking may have upon reality. Criminal law conceives of subjects-actors and then establishes connections between them of such a kind as to make it possible for the drama to be detached from its originating social circumstances and emotional roots. The drama unfolds on a stage set up by the penal system, where actors too are detached from the real persons they impersonate. Performance on this stage, however, has a peculiarity that distinguishes it from that given on any other stage: it has concrete consequences for the man of flesh-and-blood, for his lifetime and for his life and his death. Says Hulsman: "The penal system's stereotypical mode of intervention works at the level both of 'victim' and 'criminal.' Everyone receives the same treatment. All victims are supposed to have the same reactions, the same needs. The system has no regard for people in their singularity. By manifesting itself at an abstract level it hurts those it is meant to protect."[199]

The sentence delivered upon the penal stage to the abstract subject of law will be embodied in the physical and mortal person that subject represents. "Detemporalized" time is "retemporalized" during punishment. Death, which has been uncoupled from the individual, will occur either during punishment, or after it, but still the individual will die his own death. And the individual will suffer his own punishment, for abstract punishment is made manifest as concrete pain.

Legal theory also avoids reflecting on suffering. It is afraid that such reflection would compromise the purity and rigor of its rational analysis, since its only concern is to achieve a coherent and closed system. Suffering obliges us to think of the person enduring it. And this is not the subject contrived by representation but the human being of flesh and blood, who lives in the realm of doubt, in finite and uncertain time. No other experience is as intense as suffering; no other experience makes a man come face to face with himself and see himself in all his strength and weakness. Penal law knows this well; and a very bad conscience it should have for this. It is true that the apparent mitigation of the severity of punishment reflects a general sensitivity towards suffering that was not to be found before. But one wonders whether this sensitivity or revulsion towards physical punishment really is the expression of a radically changing attitude towards pain and suffering. It may equally be a sensitivity that rejects pain as spectacle, and by hiding it away, it offers fewer opportunities to react against it. This applies to the suffering both of the criminal and of the victim.

The way the issue of pain is approached is also closely linked to the way we view the relationship between society and the individual. If we see the latter as a part or fragment of society, we can apply Aquinas's analogy between the cosmos, the human body, and the body politic. "Just as in the cosmos each being is part of the whole, in the human body - a miniature cosmos - the organs are subordinated to the good of the whole. Similarly the human being is, by nature, an element of the body politic, i.e., a dependent part, subordinated to the logic of the socio-political whole. Under these conditions, just as a good physician will not hesitate to amputate an infected organ in pursuit of the body's health, it is laudable and healthy for the government to modify (through pain) or to sacrifice a dangerous individual in pursuit of the common good."[200] Here the notion of pain is linked to that of sacrifice. "Any sacrifice (understood both in a subjective and in an objective sense) is always a sacrifice in pursuit of 'something,'" says M. Scheler. And in a context relevant to our present discussion he states that only when the whole, as totality, acts, lives, and exists in all its parts, and when the parts act not only "in" but also "for" the whole, is a relationship of sacrifice between the parts and the whole genuinely possible. He defines sacrifice as follows: "An inferior element is abandoned by a superior element; the part that is abandoned suffers and dies for the whole, so that the whole may be saved, preserved and, depending on the case, benefit or grow. In all suffering, the part stands for the whole and thus prevents the greater suffering of the whole."[201] If we regard society as a whole and the individuals as its parts, and if we assign more value to the whole than to each individual part, then the suffering of the individual may be justified as a necessary sacrifice. However, if we believe, as Pareyson does, that "a person is not in society so much as in society with other persons,"[202] that is, if we reject the subordination of person to society; if we consider the existence of each person to be of equal or even greater value than the continuity of society itself, then the terms are completely reversed.

There are also other contexts in which, depending on which criterion we choose, a reflection on suffering can lead us to assume totally different positions vis-à-vis the penal problem. For instance, do we attribute a positive, educational, and strengthening value to suffering? "Zeus opened the gates of wisdom to mortals by asserting the law that knowledge is suffering."[203] Are we willing to accept the algebra of suffering: that less + less = more? On this basis, explains Pareyson, adding suffering to evil does not increase the level of negativity in the universe. It is neither a doubling nor a multiplication of evil but rather its elimination.[204] Do we really believe that in order to eliminate suffering we require additional suffering?

Our attitude in the face of suffering may explain why the victims have been for so long forgotten. As soon as we regard suffering as something positive, it follows that we should not be so concerned about repairing or mitigating a victim's pain. A likely explanation for the neglect of the victim can be found in another attitude described by Pareyson: the denunciation of evil as an affirmation of good. "Since the fatal and intrinsic self-destruction of evil already implies the institution of good, then the denouncing of evil is at once the assertion of the good: to denounce evil and to assert the good constitute a single act."[205] According to this interpretation we should be satisfied with "negating the crime as crime," believing that by "denouncing" the crime as evil the balance has been restored; it would thus be unnecessary to "do good" by taking care of the victim.

I am simply pointing out these issues to highlight the importance of reflecting upon suffering and its relationship to penal thought. The enormous depth of the subject matter, which has its roots in religious culture can, like an abyss, be disheartening. The enterprise is worth the effort, nevertheless. Penal law is trapped in a vicious circle of suffering. It originates in it and tries to rely on it for answers. And for as long as it does not reflect on suffering, it will remain unable to decide whether really it wishes to steer clear of it and finally to withdraw from the circle. To withdraw, perhaps, from penal law, and to become, as Radbruch said, "something better."

The philosophy of law claims to apply the same rigor to its reflections as scientific thought. It would rather be regarded as a "science of law." In order to achieve this goal it skirts around an extremely interesting hermeneutical task: interpreting the fantastic constructions of penal law. At the same time, it also eludes an ethical obligation: reflecting upon the implications of such constructions for the human being that suffers them.

Penal law, for its part, is more and more inclined to engage in a quest for security. This quest, the same as mere retribution, which wishes to "efface" the crime, also favours a calculative thinking which will provide it with the accuracy and certainty of empirical observation, data, and statistics. True, statistics can reveal many things. For instance, they can reveal how far we are from reaching our goals. Once we admit this fact, perhaps the most appropriate response would be to undo the journey, to walk back, to disaggregate statistics, until finally we reach the units. And then we dwell on each unit. And we reflect on each and every one of them. For each unit is the totality.

Notes

1. E. Benveniste, *Le vocabulaire des institutions indoeuropéennes* vol. 1, (Paris: Éditions de Minuit, 1969), 68.
2. E. Benveniste, «*Don et échange dans le vocabulaire indoeuropéen*», in L'Année Sociologique 2, 3 série, Paris, 1951), 8.
3. E. Benveniste, «*Don et échange dans le vocabulaire indoeuropéen*», 15.
4. V. Mathieu, *Perché punire?* (Milan: Rusconi, 1978), 126.
5. G.F.W. Hegel, *Philosophy of Right*, translated by S.W. Dyde (New York: Prometheus Books, 1996), 96.
6. F. Nietzsche, *On the Genealogy of Morals*, translated by Walter Kaufmann (New York: Vintage, 1989), 65.
7. M.M. Mackenzie, *Plato on Punishment* (Los Angeles: University of California Press 1985), 25-6.
8. M.M. Mackenzie, *Plato on Punishment*, 232.
9. E. Durkheim, "Deux lois de l'évolution pénale," *L'Année Sociologique*, series 4 (1899-1900), 90.
10. Plato, *Crito*, in *Complete Works*, ed. John M. Cooper (Indianapolis: Hackett, 1997).
11. Hegel, *Philosophy of Right*, 101.
12. E. Benveniste, *Le vocabulaire des institutions indoeuropéennes*, vol. 2, 128.
13. S. Cotta, *Perché la violenza?* (L.U. Japadre, L'Aquila, 1978), 76.
14. S. Cotta, *Perché la violenza?* 96.
15. R. Girard, *Violence and the Sacred* (Baltimore: John Hopkins University Press, 1977), 38.
16. Hegel, *Philosophy of Right*, 100.
17. «C'est le triomphe de la liberté, lorsque les lois criminelles tirent chaque peine de la nature particulière du crime. Tout l'arbitraire cesse; la peine ne descend point du caprice du législateur, mais de la nature de la chose; et ce n'est point l'homme qui fait violence à l'homme.» Montesquieu, *De l'Esprit des lois* (Paris: Garnier-Flammarion, 1979, 1, XII, chapter 4, 329. Beccaria also dedicates a chapter to the proportion between crimes and punishments.

18. C. Beccaria, *On Crimes and Punishments,* translated by David Young, Indianapolis: Hackett, 1986) 15.
19. C. Chabroud, in *Archives parlementaires,* book XXVI,618, quoted M. Foucault, *Discipline and Punish,* translated by Alan Sheridan (New York: Vintage Books, 1995), 117.
20. Foucault, *Discipline and Punish* 232.
21. Thomas Hobbes, *Leviathan,* revised student edition (Cambridge: Cambridge University Press, 2004), 218.
22. Durkheim, "Deux lois de l'évolution pénale," 83.
23. Durkheim, "Deux lois de l'évolution pénale," 83.
24. Plato, *Laws,* 908c, op. cit.; *Law,.* 908a – 908c (p. 1564).
25. Dante, *La Divina Commedia,* Inferno, Canto VI, 87, edited by D. Mattalia (Milan: Rizzoli, 1980).
26. Dante, *La Divina Commedia,* Canto IX, 27-28, note.
27. Plato, *Laws,* 909c, *op. cit.* Gernet interprets the act of throwing the criminal outside the country borders the following way: "dans le cadavre, il y a encore de la vie, il y a du pouvoir malfaisant, autrement dit du 'sacré – il y a un objet possible de deuotio: par son expulsion hors des frontières, par la destruction complete de ses restes, par le vent, l'eau et le feu, on s'efforce de l'anéantir, non pas dans un sentiment de rage pure, non pas même dans un pensée de précaution ou de défense et pour empécher un retour offensif, mais à la maniére d'un piaculum." L. Gernet, *Anthropologie de la Grèce antique* (Paris: Maspéro, 1976), 327-8.
28. L. Gernet, *Anthropologie de la Grèce antique,* 291.
29. M. Eliade, *The Sacred and the Profane,* translated by Willard R. Trask (San Diego: Harcourt Brace, 1987), 29.
30. J. Feinberg, *Doing and Deserving* (Princeton, NJ: Princeton University Press, 1970), 98.
31. S. Cotta, *Itinerari essenziali del diritto* (Naples: Morano), 135.
32. "E proprio grazie a questa generalizzazione di un primo e fondamentale aspetto dell'essistenza: la sua mancanza di innocenza." S. Cotta, *Itinerari essenziali del diritto,* 140.
33. Feinberg, *Doing and Deserving,* 115.
34. G.C. Argan, *L'arte moderna, 1770-1790* (Florence: Sansoni, 1974), 44.

35. L. Gernet, *Anthropologie de la Grèce antique*, 267.
36. L. Gernet, *Anthropologie de la Grèce antique*, 267.
37. L. Gernet, *Anthropologie de la Grèce antique*, 269.
38. C. Beccaria, *On Crimes and Punishments*, 36.
39. C. Beccaria, *On Crimes and Punishments*, 23.
40. V. Mathieu, *Perché punire?* 278.
41. Plato, *Crito*, 356a.
42. E. Benveniste, *Le vocabulaire des institutions indoeuropéennes*, vol. 2, 128.
43. A. Koyré, "*Du monde de l' «à –peu-près» à l'univers de la précision*," in *Études d'histoire de la pensée philosophique, Saint-Armand* (Paris: Gallimard), 353.
44. A. Koyré, "*Du monde de l' «à –peu-près» à l'univers de la précision*," 334, 335.
45. E. Benveniste, *Le vocabulaire des institutions indoeuropéennes*, 49.
46. Saint Augustine, *The City of God*, translated by Rev. Marcus Dods, D.D., XXI, cap. 11.
47. Saint Augustine, *The City of God*, 11.
48. Saint Augustine, *Confessions,* translated by Henry Chadwick (Oxford: Oxford University Press, 1998), XI, cap. 18, 235.
49. L. Gernet, *Anthropologie de la Grèce antique*, 289, 291.
50. V. Mathieu, *Perché punire?* 282.
51. V. Mathieu, *Perché punire?* 213.
52. Foucault, *Discipline and Punish*, 28-9.
53. Montesquieu, *De l'Esprit des lois*, 163-4.
54. M. Eliade, *The Sacred and the Profane*, 65.
55. G. Stella, *I giuristi di Husserl: L'interpretazione fenomenologica del dirito*, (Giuffré editore:, Milan, 1990), 155ff.
56. G. Stella, *I giuristi di Husserl,* 196.
57. In E. Paci's preface to the Italian version of E. Minkowski, *Le temps vécu*, (Turin: Einaudi, 1971).
58. H. Bergson, *Time and Free Will: An Essay on the Immediate Data of Consciousness*, translated by F. L. Pogson (New York: Dover Publications, 2001), 225 (*Essai sur les données inmédiates de la conscience* [Paris : Félix Alcan éditeur, 1906, 171].

59. E. Minkowski, *Le temps vécu*, 89, 92.
60. Saint Augustine, *Confessions*, 235.
61. V. Mathieu, *Perché punire?* 255.
62. For example, *Republic*, 410b
63. F. D'Agostino, *Diritto e secolarizzazione*, (Milan: Giuffré,1982), 72.
64. V. Mathieu, *Perché punire?* 16.
65. Hegel, *Philosophy of Right*, 97 and 98.
66. Hegel, *Philosophy of Right*, 98.
67. Hegel, *Philosophy of Right*, 98.
68. Saint Augustine, "Sermons", (1) S.XXXVIII.C.III.
69. M. Calvesi, "Le carceri," in Catalogue of the exhibition *Piranesi nei luoghi di Piranesi (*Rome: Mutigrafica editrice, Rome, 1979), 10.
70. M. Yourcenar, *Sous bénéfice d'inventaire* (Paris: Gallimard, 1988), 171.
71. M. Calvesi, "Le carceri," 17 ff.
72. M. Calvesi, "Le carceri," 17
73. M. Calvesi, "Le carceri," 17
74. M. Perniola, «Arte e carcere,» in *Óggi l'arte è un carcere?* edited by L. Russo (Bologna: Il Mulino, 1982), 12.
75. A. Baratta, "Viejas y nuevas estrategias de legitimización del sistema penal," *Capítulo criminológico*, no. 14 (1986), Universidad de Zulia, Maracaibo, 174 ff.
76. C. Ritschard, "*Du projet d'architecture à l'objet*," catalogue of the exhibition *Piranesi-Les vues de l'imaginaire*, (Genève: Musée Rath, 1990)
77. C. Ritschard, "*Du projet d'architecture à l'objet*,"
78. C. Beccaria, *On Crimes and Punishments*, 49.
79. C. Beccaria, *On Crimes and Punishments*, 49.
80. E.R. Zaffaroni, *En busca de las penas perdidas* (Lima: AFA editores, 1990), 226.
81. C. Beccaria, *On Crimes and Punishments*, 17.
82. C. Beccaria, *On Crimes and Punishments*, 15.
83. M. Yourcenar, *Sous bénéfice d'inventaire*, 154.
84. G. Vattimo, «Muerte y transfiguración de la metafísica,» 72.

85. M. Yourcenar, *Sous bénéfice d'inventaire* 160.
86. F. Hölderlin, quoted from *The Question concerning Technology and Other Essays* (New York: Harper & Row, 1977), 61.
87. M. Heidegger, *Being and Time*, translated by John Macquarrie and Edward Robinson (Oxford: Blackwell, 2005), 477.
88. M. Heidegger, *Being and Time*, 466.
89. M. Heidegger, *Being and Time*, 471.
90. Plato, *Filebo*, 42a, 431.
91. R.A. Guibourg, *El fenómeno normativo*, (Buenos Aires: Astrea, 1987), 30.
92. M. de Unamuno, *Tragic Sense of Life*, translated by J.E. Crawford Flitch (New York: Dover Publications, 1954).
93. A. Beristain Ipiña, *Elogio criminológico de la locura erasmiana universitaria* (Universidad del País Vasco, ed. Instituto Vasco de Criminología, San Sebastian, 1990), 12.
94. J. Carbonnier, *Sur les traces du non-sujet du droit*, in *Archive de philosophie du droit*, vol. 34, *Le sujet de droit* (Paris : Sirey, 1989), 197.
95. L. Rodríguez Manzanera, *Victimología, Estudio de la Víctima* (Mexico: Ed. Porrúa, 1990), 7.
96. L. Hulsman and J. Bernat de Celis, *Peines perdues: Le système penal en question* (Paris: Le Centurion, DHS, 1982), 135.
97. M. Heidegger, *Being and Time*, 477.
98. M. Heidegger, *Being and Time*, 115.
99. G. Capograssi, *Incertezze sull'individul* (Milan: Giuffrè, 1969), 138.
100. P. Barcellona, "I percorsi del soggetto moderno," in *IRIDE*, Filosofía e discussione publica. 18, 9 (August 1998), Florence: Il Mulino
101. C. Beccaria, *On Crimes and Punishments*, 17.
102. E.R. Zaffaroni, *En busca de las penas perdidas*, (Lima: AFA editores), 226.
103. L. Pareyson, *Ontologia della libertà*, 475-8.
104. L. Pareyson, *Dostoyevskij*, 71.
105. J. Carbonnier, *Droit et passion du Droit* (Paris : Flammarion, 1996), 147.

106. M. Foucault, *Discipline and Punish*, 74.
107.` G. Vattimo, *Etica dell'interpretazione*, 27.
108. P. Ricoeur, *The conflict of interpretations*, edited by Don Ihd (Evanston: Northwestern University Press, 2000), 358.
109. P. Ricoeur, *The conflict of interpretations*, 354
110. H.-G. Gadamer, *Truth and Method*, (1960), translated by J. Weinsheimer and D. G. Marshall (London: Continuum, 2004), 351.
111. G. Vattimo, *Beyond Interpretation*, 30.
112. G. Zaccaria, "Dimensione dell'ermeneutica e interpretazione giuridica," in *Il problema della fedeltá ermeneutica*, edited by V. Mathieu and L. Paoletti (Rome: Armando Editore, 1998), 160.
113. H.-G. Gadamer, *Truth and Method*, 277.
114. 276-7.
115. G. Zaccaria, *L'arte dell'interpretazione – Saggi sull'ermeneutica giuridica contemporanea*, (Padua: CEDAM, 1990; Zaccaria, 1990), 66.
116. H.-G. Gadamer, *Truth and Method*, 269.
117. H.-G. Gadamer, *Truth and Method*, 293- 4.
118. G. Zaccaria, *L'arte dell'interpretazione*, 109.
119. R. Alexy, *Legal Argumentation as Rational Discourse*, in "Rivista internazionale di filosofia del diritto," 4th series, 70 (1993, 2) 168.
120. G. Zaccaria, "Dimensione dell'ermeneutica e interpretazione giuridica," 151 ff.
121. R. Dworkin, *Law's Empire* (London: Fontana Press, 1986), 245.
122. G. Zaccaria, *L'arte dell'interpretazione*, 105.
123. G. Zaccaria, *L'arte dell'interpretazione*, 99ff.
124. G. Zaccaria, *L'arte dell'interpretazione*, 59.
125. H.-G. Gadamer, *Truth and Method*, 307.
126. H.-G. Gadamer, *Truth and Method*, 309.
127. G. Zaccaria, *L'arte dell'interpretazione*, 54.
128. H.-G. Gadamer, *Truth and Method*, 323.
129. H.-G. Gadamer, *Truth and Method*, 329.
130. H.-G. Gadamer, *Truth and Method*, 325-6.

131. A. Osuna Fernández Largo, *Hermenéutica jurídica: En torno a la hermenéutica jurídica de Hans-Georg Gadamer*, Universidad de Valladolid, 1992, 101.
132. H.G. Gadamer, *Reason in the Age of Science*, translated by F.G. Lawrence (Cambridge, MA: MIT Press, 2001), 126.
133. E.R. Zaffaroni, *Cronos y la aporía de la pena institucional*, in Liber ad Honorem Sergio García Ramírez, vol. 2, Universidad Nacional Autónoma de México, 1998, 1530. See also A. Miranda Rodrigues, *Temas fundamentais de execuçao penal* in Revista Brasileira de Ciências Criminais, year 6, no. 24 (Sao Paulo, 1998), 11ff.
134. A. Slokar, *El triunfo de Shylock: Algunas formulaciones sobre el alcance de la pena privativa de la libertad*, in "Revista Brasileira de Ciências Criminais," year 5, no. 19 (1997), 451.
135. R. Rorty, "Human Rights, Rationality, and Sentimentality," *The Yale Review* 81, no. 4 (October 1993).
136. E. Neuman, *No a la prisión*, in *Lecciones y Ensayos*, Abeledo Perrot, Buenos Aires, 1996, No. 66, p. 62.
137. E. Lévinas, *Quelques réflexions sur la philosophie de l'hitlerisme*, in Cahier de l'Herne, Editions de l'Herne (1991), 113.
138. Luis Fernando Niño, *La situación carcelaria en América Latina de fin de siglo y el malestar en la cultura jurídica*, in *Lecciones y Ensayos*, op. cit., 43.
139. G. Vattimo, *Etica dell'interpretazione,* 34.
140. G. Vattimo, *Etica dell'interpretazione,* 37.
141. H.G. Gadamer, *Praise of Theory: Speeches and Essays,* translated by C. Dawson (New Haven and London: Yale University Press, 1998), 57-8.
142. M. Ferraris, *History of Hermeneutics,* Trans. Luca Somigli (New Jersey: Humanity Press, 1996), 1.
143. G. Vattimo, *Beyond Interpretation*, 40.
144. Plato, *Filebo,* 758.
145. B. Romano, *Il riconoscimento come relazione giuridica fondamentale* (Rome: Bulzoni Editore, 1986), 88.
146. B. Romano, *Il riconoscimento come relazione giuridica fondamentale*, 92.

147. B. Romano, *Il riconoscimento come relazione giuridica fondamentale* 97.
148. B. Romano, *Il riconoscimento come relazione giuridica fondamentale* 99.
149. Aristotle, *Nicomachean Ethics*, translated by F. H. Peters, M. A. (New York: Barnes & Noble, 2004), 105.
150. A. Kojève, *Esquisse d'une phénomenologie du droit* (Paris : Gallimard, 1983), 75ff.
151. G. Husserl, *Diritto e tempo: Saggi di filosofia del diritto* (Milan: Giuffré Editore, 1998), 137.
152. A. Kojève, *Esquisse d'une phénomenologie du droit*, 79; G. Husserl, *Diritto e tempo: Saggi di filosofia del diritto*, 101.
153. G. Husserl, *Diritto e tempo,* 104.
154. H-G. Gadamer, *Truth and Method*, 273.
155. H-G. Gadamer, *Truth and Method*, 278.
156. H-G. Gadamer, *Truth and Method*, 355.
157. Saint Augustine, *Confessions*, XI, 26, 235.
158. F. Ost, *Le Temps du Droit* (Paris : Editions Odile Jacob, 1999), 338.
159. F. Ost, *Le Temps du Droit*, 120.
160. P. Legendre, *Law and the Unconscious: A Legendre Reader* (London: Macmillan Press, 1997), 189.
161. H-G. Gadamer, *Truth and Method*, 269.; see also Zaccaria, *Questioni di interpretazione* (Padua: Cedam, 1996) 68 ff.
162. G. Husserl, *Diritto e tempo,* 16.
163. H-G. Gadamer, *Truth and Method*, 297.
164. H-G. Gadamer, *Truth and Method*, 316.
165. H-G. Gadamer, *Truth and Method*, 27
166. H-G. Gadamer, *Truth and Method*, 27-8; see also F. Viola and G. Zaccaria, *Diritto e interpretazione* (Bari: Editori Laterza, 1999), 448.
167. P. Ricoeur, *The Just,* translated by D. Pellauer (Chicago: The University of Chicago Press, 2000), 154.
168. J. Derrida, "Diritto alla Giustizia," in *Diritto, Giustizia e Interpretazione,* edited by J. Derrida and G. Vattimo (Laterza, Bari: Annuario Filosofico Europeo, 1998), 23.

169. G. Zaccaria, *L'arte dell'interpretazione-Saggi sull'ermeneutica giuridica contemporanea* (Padua: Cedam, 1990), 87ff.; also see Gadamer, op. cit., 329.
170. Gadamer, *Reason in the Age of Science*, 126.
171. Zaccaria, *Questioni di interpretazione*, 15; see also F. Viola and G. Zaccaria, *Diritto e interpretazione* 205.
172. Gadamer, *The Ideal of Practical Philosophy*, 58.
173. J. Carbonnier, *Flexible Droit*, Librarie Générale de droit et jurisprudence (Paris: E.J.A. 1992), 361.
174. B. Romano, *Il riconoscimento come relazione giuridica fondamentale* (Rome: Bulzoni Editore, 1986), 239.
175. B. Romano, *Il riconoscimento come relazione giuridica fondamentale* 117.
176. F. Nietzsche, *On the Genealogy of Morals*, translated by Walter Kaufmann and R. J. Hollingdale (New York: Vintage, 1989), 58.
177. M. Heidegger, *Off the Beaten Track* (1950), translated by J. Young and K. Haynes (Cambridge: Cambridge University Press, 2002), 69 and 70.
178. G. Stella, *I giuristi di Husserl* (Milan: Giuffrè Editore, 1990), 155.
179. S. Cotta, *Il diritto nell'esistenza* (Milan: Giuffrè Editore, 1984), 181 ff.
180. L. Pareyson, *Esistenza e persona,* 181ff.
181. G. Husserl, *Diritto e tempo, Saggi di filosofia del diritto* (Milan:Giuffrè Editore, 1998), 57.
182. F. Nietzsche, *Thus Spoke Zarathustra*, translated by Walter Kaufmann (The Modern Library, New York, 1995), 140.
183. M. Heidegger, *What Is Called Thinking,* translated by J. Glenn Gray (New York: Harper, 1968), 103.
184. M. Heidegger, *What Is Called Thinking,* 103; See E. R. Zaffaroni, "Qué pena," in *Fascículos de Ciências Penais,* year 5, vol. 5 no. 3 July/August/September 1992.
185. G. Husserl, *Diritto e tempo,* 57.
186. G. Husserl, *Diritto e tempo,* 160.
187. Hegel, *Philosophy of Right*, 95.

188. P. Ricoeur, *The conflict of Interpretations*, 354.
189. P. Ricoeur, *The conflict of Interpretations*, 358.
190. P. Ricoeur, *The conflict of Interpretations*, 362.
191. G. Husserl, *Diritto e tempo*, 52.
192. Hegel, *Philosophy of Right*, 101.
193. P. Ricoeur, *The Just*, 133.
194. Kojève, *Esquisse d'une phénomenologie du droit*, 69ff.
195. S. Cotta, «Quidquid latet apparebit: Le problême de la verité du jugement,» *Archivio di filosofia* 56, nos. 1-3 (1988) : 395.
196. Kojève, *Esquisse d'une phénomenologie du droit*, 420ff.
197. B. Romano, *Ortonomia della relazione giuridica: Una filosofia del diritto*, (Rome: Bulzoni Editore, 1997), 33.
198. L. Pareyson, *Ontologia della libertà*, 156.
199. L. Hulsman and J. Bernat de Celis, *Peines perdues, le système penal en question* (Paris : Le centurion, DHS, 1982), 94.
200. G. Courtois, «Le sens de la douleur chez Saint Thomas,» in *La Douleur et le droit*, edited by B. Durand, J. Poirier, Jean-Pierre Royer (Press Universitaires de France, 1997), 105 ff.
201. M. Scheler, *Le sens de la souffrance* suivi de deux autres essais *Repentir et renaissance, Amour et connaissance* (Paris: Aubier, 1951) 14.
202. L. Pareyson, *Esistenza e persona*, 192.
203. G. Cupido, "Pathos e mathos nel mondo tragico sofocleo," in *Iride, Filosofia e discussione pubblica* 17, year 9 (April 1996) (Bologna: Il Mulino), 189.
204. L. Pareyson, "Ontologia della libertà," op. cit., 477.
205. L. Pareyson, *Dostoyevsky*, 71 ff.

Bibliography

Alexy, R. "*Legal Argumentation as Rational Discourse*", en Rivista internazionale di filosofia del diritto, 4th series, 70, 1993.

Argan, G.C. *L'arte moderna, 1770-1790*, Florence: Sansoni, 1974.

Aristotle, *Nicomachean Ethics*, translated by F. H. Peters, New York: Barnes & Noble, 2004.

Baratta, A, "Viejas y nuevas estrategias de legitimización del sistema penal," in *Capítulo criminológico*, no. 14, 1986.

Barcellona, P. "I percorsi del soggetto moderno," in *IRIDE*, Filosofía e discussione publica. 18, 1998.

Beccaria, C. *On Crimes and Punishments*, translated by David Young, Indianapolis: Hackett, 1986.

Benveniste, E, *Le vocabulaire des institutions indoeuropéennes*, vol. 1, Paris: Les éditions de minuit, 1969)

Benveniste, E, «*Don et échange dans le vocabulaire indoeuropéen*,» in *L'Année Sociologique*, series 3 (1948-1949), pp. 7-20. Reprinted in E. Benveniste, *Problèmes de linguistique générale*, Paris, Gallimard, 1966, t. I, pp. 315-327.

Bergson, H, *Time and Free Will: An Essay on the Immediate Data of Consciousness*, translated by F. L. Pogson, New York: Dover Publications, 2001.

Beristain Ipiña, A. *Elogio criminológico de la locura erasmiana universitaria* (Universidad del País Vasco, San Sebastian: ed. Instituto Vasco de Criminología, 1990

Calvesi, M, *Le carceri*, Catalogue of the exhibition *Piranesi nei luoghi di Piranesi,* Mutigrafica editrice, Rome, 1979.

Capograssi, G. *Incertezze sull'individul*, Milan: Giuffrè, 1969.

Carbonnier, J. *Sur les traces du non-sujet du droit*, in *Archive de philosophie du droit*, vol. 34, *Le sujet de droit*, Paris : Sirey, 1989.

Carbonnier, J. *Droit et passion du Droit*, Paris : Flammarion, 1996.

Carbonnier, J. *Flexible Droit*, Paris: E.J.A. 1992.

Chabroud, C, in *Archives parlementaires*, book XXVI,618, in M. Foucault, *Discipline and Punish*, translated by Alan Sheridan, New York: Vintage Books, 1995.

Cotta, S. *Itinerari essenziali del diritto* (Naples: Morano), 135.

Cotta, S, *Perché la violenza?* L'Aquila: L.U. Japadre, 1978.

Cotta, S. *Il diritto nell'esistenza*, Milan: Giuffrè Editore, 1984.

Cotta, S. "Quidquid latet apparebit: Le problême de la verité du jugement," *Archivio di filosofia* 56, nos. 1-3, 1988.

Courtois, G. "Le sens de la douleur chez Saint Thomas," in *La Douleur et le droit*, edited by B. Durand, J. Poirier, Jean-Pierre Royer Paris: Press Universitaires de France, 1997.

Cupido, G. «Pathos e mathos nel mondo tragico sofocleo,» in *Iride, Filosofia e discussione pubblica* 17, year 9, 1996.

D'Agostino, F, *Diritto e secolarizzazione*, Milan: Giuffré,1982.

Dante, *La Divina Commedia*, edited by D. Mattalia, Milan: Rizzoli, 1980.

Derrida, J. "Diritto alla Giustizia," in *Diritto, Giustizia e Interpretazione*, edited by J. Derrida and G. Vattimo, Roma-Bari: Laterza, 1998.

de Unamuno, M. *Tragic Sense of Life*, translated by J.E. Crawford Flitch, New York: Dover Publications, 1954

Durkheim, E, "Deux lois de l'évolution pénale," in *L'Année Sociologique*, series 4, 1899-1900.

Dworkin, R. *Law's Empire*, London: Fontana Press, 1986.

Eliade, M, *The Sacred and the Profane*, translated by Willard R. Trask, San Diego: Harcourt Brace, 1987.

Feinberg, J. *Doing and Deserving*, Princeton, NJ: Princeton University Press, 1970.

Ferraris, M, *History of Hermeneutics*, Trans. Luca Somigli, New Jersey: Humanity Press, 1996.

Gadamer, H.-G. *Truth and Method*, (1960), translated by J. Weinsheimer and D. G. Marshall, London: Continuum, 2004

Gadamer, H.G. *Reason in the Age of Science*, translated by F.G. Lawrence, Cambridge, MA: MIT Press, 2001.

Gadamer, H.G. *Praise of Theory: Speeches and Essays,* translated by C. Dawson, (New Haven and London: Yale University Press, 1998.

Gernet, L. *Anthropologie de la Grèce antique*, Paris: Maspéro, 1976

Girard, R. *Violence and the Sacred*, Baltimore: John Hopkins University Press, 1977.

Guibourg, R.A. *El fenómeno normativo*, Buenos Aires: Astrea, 1987

Hegel, G.F.W. *Philosophy of Right*, translated by S.W. Dyde, New York: Prometheus Books, 1996.

Heidegger, M. *Being and Time*, translated by John Macquarrie and Edward Robinson, Oxford: Blackwell, 2005

Heidegger, M. *Off the Beaten Track* (1950), translated by J. Young and K. Haynes Cambridge: Cambridge University Press, 2002.

Heidegger, M. *What Is Called Thinking,* translated by J. Glenn Gray, New York: Harper, 1968

Hobbes, T, *Leviathan,* Cambridge: Cambridge University Press, 2004.

Hölderlin, F. quoted from M. Heidegger, *The Question concerning Technology and Other Essays*, New York: Harper & Row, 1977

Hulsman L, and J. Bernat de Celis, *Peines perdues: Le système penal en question*, Paris: Le Centurion, DHS, 1982.

Husserl, G. *Diritto e tempo: Saggi di filosofia del diritto*, Milan: Giuffré Editore, 1998.

Kojève, A, *Esquisse d'une phénomenologie du droit*, Paris : Gallimard, 1983.

Koyré, A, *Du monde de l' «à –peu-près» à l'univers de la précision,* in *Études d'histoire de la pensée philosophique, Saint-Armand,* Paris: Gallimard, 1971.

Legendre, P. *Law and the Unconscious: A Legendre Reader,* London: Macmillan Press, 1997.

Lévinas, E. *Quelques réflexions sur la philosophie de l'hitlerisme,* in Cahier de l'Herne, Editions de l'Herne, 1991.

Mackenzie, M.M. *Plato on Punishment,* Los Angeles: University of California Press 1985.

Mathieu, M, *Perché punire?* Milan: Rusconi, 1978.

Miranda Rodrigues, A, "*Temas fundamentais de execuçao penal*" in Revista Brasileira de Ciências Criminais, year 6, no. 24 (Sao Paulo, 1998.

Montesquieu, *De l'Esprit des lois,* Paris: Garnier-Flammarion, 1979.

Neuman, E, *No a la prisión,* in *Lecciones y Ensayos,* Abeledo Perrot, Buenos Aires, 1996, No. 66

Nietzsche, F. *Thus Spoke Zarathustra,* translated by Walter Kaufmann, New York: The Modern Library, 1995.

Nietzsche, F, *On the Genealogy of Morals,* translated by Walter Kaufmann, New York: Vintage, 1989.

Ost, F. *Le Temps du Droit,* Paris : Editions Odile Jacob, 1999.

Osuna Fernández Largo, A. *Hermenéutica jurídica: En torno a la hermenéutica jurídica de Hans-Georg Gadamer,* Valladolid: Universidad de Valladolid, 1992.

Paci, E. "Preface" to the Italian version of E. Minkowski, *Le temps vécu,* Turin: Einaudi, 1971.

Pareyson, L. *Ontologia della libertà, Il male e la sofferenza,* Turin: Einaudi, 1995

Pareyson, L. *Dostoyevskij, Filosofia, romanzo ed esperienza religiosa,* Turin: Einaudi, 1993.

Pareyson, L. *Esistenza e persona, il melangolo*, Turin, 1992.

Perniola, P, "Arte e carcere," in *Oggi l'arte è un carcere?* edited by L. Russo, Bologna: Il Mulino, 1982.

Plato, *Crito*, in *Complete Works*, ed. John M. Cooper, Indianapolis: Hackett, 1997.

Plato, *Laws*, 908.

Ricoeur, P. *The conflict of interpretations*, edited by Don Ihd (Evanston: Northwestern University Press, 2000.

Ricoeur, P. *The Just,* translated by D. Pellauer, Chicago: The University of Chicago Press, 2000.

Ritschard, C. "*Du projet d'architecture à l'objet*," catalogue of the exhibition *Piranesi-Les vues de l'imaginaire*, Genève, 1990, Musée Rath.

Rodríguez Manzanera, L. *Victimología, Estudio de la Víctima*, Mexico: Ed. Porrúa, 1990.

Romano, B. *Il riconoscimento come relazione giuridica fondamentale*, Rome: Bulzoni Editore, 1986.

Romano, B. *Ortonomia della relazione giuridica: Una filosofia del diritto*, Rome: Bulzoni Editore, 1997.

Rorty, R. "Human Rights, Rationality, and Sentimentality," in *The Yale Review* 81, no. 4 October 1993.

Saint Augustine, *The City of God*, translated by Rev. Marcus Dods, Published in 1886 by Philip Schaff, New York: Christian Literature Publishing Co.

Saint Augustine, *Confessions,* translated by Henry Chadwick, Oxford: Oxford University Press, 1998.

Scheler, M, *Le sens de la souffrance* suivi de deux autres essais *Repentir et renaissance, Amour et connaissance*, Paris: Aubier, 1951.

Slokar, A. "*El triunfo de Shylock: Algunas formulaciones sobre el alcance de la pena privativa de la libertad*," in Revista Brasileira de Ciências Criminais, year 5, no. 19, 1997.

Stella, G. *I giuristi di Husserl: L'interpretazione fenomenologica del dirito*, Milan: Giuffré editore, 1990.

Vattimo, G. "Muerte y transfiguración de la metafísica," *Revista de Occidente*, no. 102 November 1989.

Vattimo, G. *Etica dell'interpretazione,* Turin: Rosenberg & Sellier, 1989.

Vattimo, G. *Beyond Interpretation: The Meaning of Hermeneutics for Philosophy*, translated by D. Webb, Cambridge: Polity Press, 1997.

Viola F. and G. Zaccaria, *Diritto e interpretazione*, Roma-Bari: Editori Laterza, 1999.

Yourcenar, M, *Sous bénéfice d'inventaire*, Paris: Gallimard, 1988.

Zaccaria, G. *Dimensione dell'ermeneutica e interpretazione giuridica*, in *Il problema della fedeltá ermeneutica*, edited by V. Mathieu and L. Paoletti, Rome: Armando Editore, 1998, 143-170.

Zaccaria, G. *L'arte dell'interpretazione – Saggi sull'ermeneutica giuridica contemporanea*, Padua: CEDAM, 1990; Zaccaria, 1990.

Zaccaria, G. *Questioni di interpretazione*, Padua: Cedam, 1996.

Zaffaroni, E.R. *En busca de las penas perdidas*, Lima: AFA editores, 1990

Zaffaroni, E.R. *Cronos y la aporía de la pena institucional*, in Liber ad Honorem Sergio García Ramírez, vol. 2, Universidad Nacional Autónoma de México, 1998.

Zaffaroni, E. R. "Qué pena," in *Fascículos de Ciências Penais,* year 5, vol. 5 no. 3 July/August/September 1992.

Made in the USA
Monee, IL
04 November 2026

67374679R00069